Just
After
Inca

Just After Inca

ONE WOMAN'S JOURNEY
THROUGH INCEST
TO HEALING

BY REBECCA BASS

THE CROSSING PRESS
FREEDOM, CA 95019

Library of Congress Cataloging-in-Publication Data

Bass, Rebecca.
    Just after Inca: one woman's journey through incest to healing:
a novel / by Rebecca Bass.
          p. cm.
      ISBN 0-89594-538-X : ISBN 0-89594-537-1 (pbk.)
      I. Title.
    PS3552.A82128J87 1992
    813'.54—dc20   91-43203
                                                     CIP

To:

Betty Glotfelty Hummel, M.A.

1

At the end of a hot dusty day, I walked down the uneven cement street, head down, pondering the deep paths cut into the weeds instead of the sidewalks I had known on my side of town. I didn't see the little girl standing next to my old VW until I crossed around to the driver's side.

Light-skinned, her head seemed to have been surveyed to have gotten the parts in perfect squares and the little braids so perfectly centered in every square. Each braid, no bigger than a pencil, had a little blue plastic barrette the color of her starched dress at the end of each tuft. Her eyes matched the color of her dress, a shade of blue I have never again seen in eyes. She stood still, then extended her hand to offer me a piece of writing paper.

I thanked her, then opened the little pebbled page to read the fern-delicate handwriting. It said: "The woman you are looking for, Martha Waters, will be waiting for you at 664 Sugah Hill Street at 4:00 tomorrow afternoon." I looked up to thank the child, to tell her I'd be there, but she had disappeared into one of the houses. Not a single person was on any of the porches.

Driving to the top of the hill to turn around, I went slowly, looking for house numbers. Not many houses had them, but I found 664 and thought for a moment that I saw the little blue-eyed girl behind the faint movement of a curtain. Then the curtain closed.

Here I was, taking time from my master's program, involved in the beginnings of the civil rights movement. Brash as only a twenty-four year old can be, I had gone to my own home town to register voters.

Since Sugah Hill was the area of town with the most black people, that's where I started, talking to the folks who lived in the shanties about registering. I'd stand on the rickety porches and talk to the women of the house, always the women. Black men on the Hill would never be seen talking to a white woman, at least no black man who values his balls. I'd say my spiel about voting being a right that the Constitution gave all people and would urge the women to go down to the court house and register, offering to take them if they'd go.

They would stand there on one foot, the other propped akimbo on a knee, leaning on an unpainted wall, most with a dip of snuff the size of a grape tucked into their bottom lip. Almost every person I talked to was fifty or older and almost every woman knew my grandfather. The women would never look me directly in the eye; black people of that age who didn't work in the homes of white people never did. They'd nod, moving their whole upper body in agreement with every statement I made. Finished with my registration talk, I'd leave my leaflets and pamphlets, then I'd ask my other questions, the ones about Aunt Martha.

"Yazz'm, Aunt Marfa Waters still alive."

"No'm, nobody heah know wheah she lib."

I would move on to the the next house, sensing dark eyes following my every move, dreading my arrival.

Now the blue-eyed girl had delivered the answer I'd been looking for. Aunt Martha was not only still alive, she had invited me to come visit the next day! The vein in my throat throbbed with anticipation. There'd be no more registration calls that day. I had to buy her a wonderful present before the stores closed.

I agonized over the gift. It would have to be pristine, the very best of its kind money could buy. It had to tell her how many times I had cuddled up to her in my dreams for safety, how much I had missed her, how sorry I was that I hadn't searched for her sooner. It would have to be a vessel carrying all the love I was bringing her.

I wandered along the sidewalks looking into the windows of the sorry little shops, seeing with new eyes what a dirt-water town it was. "Don't rise above your upbringing, girl," my mind whispered to itself.

I turned into Eve's. She had lots of cut glass and new brass and the nicest furniture in town. She even had a room full of what passed in the town as antiques.

Eve's husband had abandoned her and his middle-management job at the pulp mill to run off with a girl half his age, a former head majorette in the high school marching band. Evelyn had managed to keep her head up and her mind busy by opening her shop. All the salaried people in town agreed that she had very good taste. She had helped with the interior decoration of many of the managers' houses.

I walked into the back room and looked at the lackluster trinkets and odd pieces of china. Almost half way around, beginning to despair, I spied a cobalt blue glass vase with a fluted top about six inches high. When I picked it up I saw USA-2 in raised letters on the bottom. Ridges with glass nobs ran down the body of the vase.

"I'm gonna have to get five dollars for that, honey." I hadn't seen Eve come into the room, but there she was, standing at my elbow. I realized later that she probably thought anyone working with "the nigras" would probably steal. She had to protect her extensive investment. I must have hesitated too long.

"They're not making cobalt glass anymore, honey. Five dollars is the lowest I can go on that." I held the vase up to the light to look for cracks and ran my finger around the top to be sure it wasn't broken. "It's fine, honey," Eve assured me. "Everything in the shop is perfect, just like your grandmother had it."

Did I hear sarcasm? I looked at her with renewed interest, surprised that anything cynical or in the least questioning could survive in my home town. I gave her five dollars from my purse, knowing she'd probably be hesitant to take a check from me.

Leggatt's was where any girl who'd been shaving under her arms for more than five years went to buy wedding silver and china. They would ogle the merchandise on the black velvet trays in the glass display case. In teenageese this merchandise was known generically as "diamonds," never as "engagement rings" or simply "rings."

Mr. Leggatt extended credit to boys who had their first paycheck from the mill, guiding their selection by showing them a picture of the ring in a bridal magazine, letting them look at it through his ocular piece. If the girl came with him for the selection process, Mr. Leggatt made the occasion more memorable than her wedding or her honeymoon, surely more memorable than losing her virginity to some clumsy mill hand. Usually the easy terms Mr. Leggatt exacted lasted past the toilet training of the couple's first child.

I was glad to see Mrs. Leggatt in the store. A tall stringy woman, her skin was sallow, stretched across the enlarged knuckles of her hands, making them look like bird's feet. She usually stayed in the back of the shop to repair the crystals and overextended springs of the Waltham and Helbros watches the store featured. She also did engraving, with chisels so small they hardly seemed like tools at all.

I looked at silver trays and bowls, not even close to what I wanted. I hardly glanced at the watches; the last thing an old woman wanted was a calibration of her remaining hours.

A grey velvet card displaying silver charms caught my eye. "I'd like to see those," I told her.

She smiled and set the card on top of the display case. Reaching beneath it for more, she said, "We hardly get any call for these anymore since the girls don't wear charm bracelets today. I can give you a good price on either the gold or the silver."

By the time she'd finished she had hundreds of gold and silver charms on top of the case and I was feeling pressure to choose something. "Take your time," she said, sensing my tension.

And then I saw it: a silver half-moon with the face of a woman. It was perfect, wonderfully dreamy in design, Art Nouveau-looking, as if designed by Aubrey Beardsley. A jump ring allowed for wearing on a chain as a necklace.

Mrs. Leggatt was not one to gush over the choices of customers; that was for her husband. "Can I get you a chain for that?" she asked simply, already buffing it with jeweler's rouge. The moon was shining in her hand.

"No chain," I said.

She put the moon in a little white cardboard box over pressed cotton fluff, and I paid her, smiling as I left.

I bought a yard of silk cord, a rich reddish purple, from a fabric shop on my way to the florist on Washington Street. I tried to see what kinds of flowers were hidden in the large glass cooler, but the work table obscured my view.

A dowdy little woman with an ornate French twist stepped up to the counter. "Carnations today?" she asked. "Or roses?"

"No, I'm looking for something more exotic."

"Oh. More exotic," she mimicked as closely as she dared.

"Do you have any orchids?"

"Yes, we do." The set of her jaw and the line of her mouth told me she'd show me.

She lifted the hinged barrier of the counter, beckoning me into the back room. "We're getting ready for a fancy 'piscopal wedding and we just got these in. We can sell you whatever you want." She put her hand under the sensuous lip of a white one. "This would make you a lovely corsage. It'd go with anything."

When I spied the one I wanted, I took the silk cord from its bag and held it over to the flower. The pale yellow of the petals would be lovely in the blue vase, with the reddish purple lip exactly matching the color of the silk cord.

"That cord is gonna be hell to work with. We like to use our own ribbon." She sensed encroachment into her domain, a demand she didn't want to meet. Her mouth was a line again.

"I don't want a corsage," I told her evenly. "I want to put it in a vase."

"Then we'll deliver it in a vase," she said, in charge again.

"Actually, I'd like it in one of those little vials that keep it fresh. And in a box. I'll pick it up myself about 3:30 tomorrow." I had my wallet out and showed her a twenty.

Seeing the money made it easier. She waved her hand at a wire rack of tiny cards. "Take your pick," she said. "We'll just tuck it into the box beside the bloom."

I sighed at the thought of telling her I didn't want a card and that the person, negro, receiving it couldn't read. But I chose one and wrote on it, "Much love, Becca." I could take it out of the box later.

Walking back toward my car I noticed Dr. Grey's old office and jaywalked across the street to look inside. I could smell his old parrot in the cage without opening the door. Under a big sign — "This parrot *will bite*" — was posted a schedule of the doctor's abbreviated hours. So the old man was still alive, still working. Dark golden rivulets of solidified nicotine on the walls said that he was also still smoking.

Across the street at the drug store I sat in a teen-scarred booth. Waiting for my coke, I thought about the doctor. There had been a problem with one of Aunt Martha's kin, maybe a daughter, maybe a niece. She lay up in one of the shanties on Sugah Hill screaming from the baby she couldn't birth. Someone had gone through the rain to get the doctor, but he was a young man then, just married and randy as a buck goat. When he rolled out of bed in the morning and remembered the woman on Sugah Hill it was too late. She had bled to death.

It was easy enough for Aunt Martha to get some of the dead woman's blood, since the shanty seemed awash with it. Besides, it didn't take much; as everyone knows, nothing is as strong as birthing blood. A small curl of the woman's hair was collected, too, soaked as it was with sweat. Finally she took parings of the dead woman's nails, putting them with the rest in a clean snuff box for later use.

Aunt Martha waited until spring to collect the plant for roots to read on Dr. Grey. She dug a bloodroot so carefully she got every tiny hair root, rinsing it carefully in the rain water captured in the gallon canning jar she had placed under the cement cross on her cousin's grave. She went to a high place in the swamp — she called it a hammock — to dig the manroot that grew there, washing it too in the water that had dripped from the cement cross.

By this time everyone on Sugah Hill had heard of her efforts, even some of the white people who believed in readings and spells. The whole community seemed to be holding its collective breath.

They had never heard of a reading so strong, or a spell that would be so powerful.

When Dr. Grey's first child was born, they waited to hear what would befall his woman and his child. To everyone's amazement, mother and daughter were both fine.

Before his daughter was two years old, word spread that his wife was pregnant again. Aunt Martha made a small altar on the highboy in her room. Taking the bloodroot and the manroot out of their separate jars she put them together in a jar with the fresh rainwater. Into the water also went a tiny strand of the dead woman's hair, a shaving of her toenail, and some of the dried birthing blood. Word spread of this, too. Everyone who heard of the ceremonies on Aunt Martha's altar trembled, whether they believed in readings or not.

Dr. Grey's son seemed healthy enough at birth, but he appeared bruised and bluer with each passing day. The doctor knew the son he had dreamed about, had fantasized about sending to Wake Forest medical school in his footsteps, was a hemophiliac the moment he had laid eyes on him. He let his black house help go and hired white maids at twice the cost. He was afraid the old black sorceress had bewitched all the negroes and they would make his son bleed.

The sight of the doctor's office, the feel of the drug store, the happiness of finding Aunt Martha, conspired to take my attention off the registration drive. I couldn't help thinking of my own beginnings in that town, and of what came later...

The walls were a shiny, glossy green, not uncommon for the time. From a Bakelite rosette in the middle of the ceiling hung an enameled metal shade, deflecting harsh light from a naked bulb. The cotton sheets, lightly starched and ironed, seemed to stretch forever in the glaring light. They smelled of lavender from the linen press in the hall.

I was awake now, but couldn't locate myself on the bed again, lost on the counterpane. The bed yawned like the Sahara as I extended my hand, trying to find the edge of the mattress. When my fingers touched the piping under the top sheet I knew I had found it. My hand became the only part of my body normal sized. The rest of me felt puny, diminished by the normality of my hand.

I whimpered for a few seconds and was at full throat by the time Aunt Martha got to me. Mother was gone again, off on the 3 o'clock train to St. Louis.

Aunt Martha wrapped me in a quilt like a little mummy and carried me, my nostrils full of her pheromones and not my mother's, through the dark halls to the kitchen. She sat me deep into a rump-sprung upholstered rocking chair with arms carved like swans' heads.

She needed to make the fire to fry the rashers of smoked bacon and slabs of salty ham, thick as a hand. Taking two thin sticks of light'rd the color of a brick, so full of pitch they seemed to want to explode in her hand, she laid them in the firebox of the big iron cookstove, on top of kindling split by trustees on icy mornings. The big hardwood billets that would smoulder and burn slowly she handled as easily as she had lifted me. Aunt Martha was strong for a little woman.

Aunt Martha rose first in the house, the self-appointed guardian of the woodpile, since she started the cooking fire. She would never trust fire-building to Cap'n LL's wife, the supervisor of the County Home, or to the white slatterns living down on the white inmate wings, working off their sentences for bad checks or prostitution. They didn't know nothin' 'bout work.

"White womens don't know nothin' 'bout fire," she muttered under her breath in the patois with which she buffered herself when white women were actually present. She glanced at the swan chair and me, my eyelids twitching in pretended sleep as I watched her. "I know you ain't sleepin', chile. You cain't fool your Aunt Marfa."

I screwed my eyes shut, blocking out her wavering image and all the light, listening as she swept the head of the big wooden match along the metal side of the stove, smelling the sulfur as it flared. "You ain't lightin' no more matches, chile, not in de stove or nowhere."

8

"Yes, ma'm," I told her, and that was the end of that. She would never again bring up the fire I had started in the back garden though she had been blamed for it.

I knew Grandmother had talked hard to her about teaching me to strike matches and light the kitchen fire. She was the one who'd found me out near the vegetable garden, standing beside a patch of blackened stubble watching a merry line of flames licking its way toward the back wing of the Home. It was all she and Crazy Joe could do to get it out. There had been no trustees around to help. They'd all been working over at the prison kitchen. The inmates in the back wing were all bedridden, in wheelchairs or otherwise too infirm to beat out fire with blankets.

When the fire was finally out, Grandmother sat on the cement steps of the back porch, fanning herself with her apron. Crazy Joe just couldn't light, but bobbed and hopped and pulled at his grizzled hair, mumbling to himself. Grandmother took him by the hand and sat him down beside her, stroking and patting his back and neck as she would a puppy until he was calm.

Grandmother's name was Cornelia Barnes Bass. She was the wife of Luther Lorenzo Bass, and supervisor of the Washington County Home for the Indigent. Though overweight and hypertensive she gave the appearance of a robust woman. Stepping lightly over the matches scattered on the ground, she picked me up from the other side of the burned area. "Joe, see to the matches, please."

Her voice was so unlike her demeanor: honking, loud, in a register assaulting the sensibilities of the listener. It was the voice of a deaf person. She watched to see that he understood. "You are going to your room, Miss Priss," she finger-spelled to the child.

"I'm sorry, Grandmother, I'm sorry," I spelled back.

I lay on my bed now, watching the organdy curtains move against their own folds into endless patterns of crosshatching. "If I start another fire she'll hang me on the curtain frames," I tried to tell myself, knowing even as I thought it it wasn't true. Sending me to my room was the harshest punishment Grandmother had ever exacted for my misdeeds. Curtains were the only thing she would hang on the frames.

Aunt Martha washed the curtains every month in the summertime. The soot from the troop trains was drawn through the open windows with the breeze, every dark speck magnified on the gossamer fabric.

Aunt Martha and Grandmother had three iron pots out back. The really big one was for rendering lard during winter hog-killing time and for making the hominy. None of the family liked hominy, white and doughy as it was, like fat people's toes. Lots of the inmates, black and white, liked it though. "There's no accounting for taste," Grandmother would spell as she heaped the metamorphasized corn into bowls dotted with dollops of melting butter.

A smaller pot, holding about seven gallons, was the soap pot. Scared to death that I'd get into the Red Devil lye, Aunt Martha and Grandmother saved the ashes from the hickory burned in the big cook stove; water dripping through the hickory ashes made the lye. Then on Monday, when Aunt Martha and the maids washed the clothes out back, Aunt Martha would drip the lye for soap and hominy.

She'd mix the lye water with the grease she'd saved from cooking, boiling the mixture in the soap pot until it looked like jelly. Then she'd pour the mixture into an enameled pan to congeal and harden. The soap that formed was as amber as traders' beads and fierce in its strength against soil.

One of the maids — not just a run-of-the-mill prostitute, but a real fancy woman — once hurt Aunt Martha's feelings by asking her to make the soap smell better. Aunt Martha knew very well which leaves to add for sweetness, how to add the little brown wild ginger calyxes for a spicy smell. For her, cleansing both body and possessions bordered on a sacred act. Such ablutions were not to be diminished by frivolity and scented soap.

Aunt Martha cast a spell on the fancy woman. I knew she was going to when I saw her collecting the woman's hair from the bathtub drain. I saw Aunt Martha slip, quiet as moonlight, down the cement steps out back and out into the pasture where they buried the inmates who died with no one to take them to a family plot. I saw her crouch to go through the strands of barbed wire keeping the stock out of the graveyard, but I couldn't see what she did.

Within a week of Aunt Martha's sojourn to the graveyard the fancy lady developed a raised angry-looking ridge on the inside of her arm. "Ringworm," Grandmother diagnosed.

Dr. Grey, who visited the county home to check on everyone twice a month and more often when he was called, agreed. "The best thing in the world for that ringworm'd be that lye soap that Aunt Martha and Miz LL makes out back," he told the fancy lady. "You wouldn't want that ol' thing to get into that pretty hair of yours, now would you, hon?" He stroked her hair and she tucked her chin onto her chest, looking upward at him. He stroked her hair again. "A woman's hair is her beauty. Says so in the Bible."

"But it *smells* so bad," the fancy lady said petulantly, sticking out her bottom lip in a way that would have earned me an afternoon in my room with no Sears and Roebuck catalog to break the monotony.

He removed his hand from her hair. Though he had never hit a lick of real work his hands were hard, thumb and forefinger completely stained yellow from the cigarette that was his constant companion. His hand lingered on her bosom, fondling it through her cotton work shirt. She beamed at him, her chin still on her chest. When she cut her eyes over to where I stood watching, she gave him a meaningful look.

He moved his hand, chuckling under his breath. "Use that soap on your hair as a prophylactic, hon. You know what a prophylactic is. I don't have to tell YOU that. If ringworm gets into that mane of yours, we'll either have to shave it or every strand'll fall out. Either way, you'll be just as bald as a cue ball."

He reached for her again, but remembering my presence, dropped his hand. "Nobody likes bald pussy, honey, 'cept on really little girls." They glanced my way and laughed.

Past them, through the door, I saw Aunt Martha's dusky form. I knew that huge devilment was afoot. She'd never let the fancy woman get away with yet another slight. The white whore would have hell to pay.

Aunt Martha had already read the roots on Dr. Grey. Though everyone in town knew it, I only learned about it after Aunt Martha was a very old woman, no longer working for white folks.

2

The county home and the prison farm behind it were both served by the meat and produce raised by the prisoners. Grandfather Bass — Cap'n LL to most, or simply Cap'n — was both sheriff of the county and warden of the prison farm.

The farm was worked by prisoners, who took care of butchering the beef and slaughtering the hogs. Those who rose to the rank of trustee kept smoke in the smokehouse and saw to the curing of the salt meat. I helped by keeping a sharp eye out for the skipper fly, whose larva ruined meat.

The prisoners in the fields worked in gangs of eight or ten, each watched by a guard with a double-barreled shotgun. For every group of three or four gangs there was an extra guard with a deer rifle, but I can remember only twice hearing it shot. The shotguns could usually take care of most of the business for which guns were needed.

A big Jersey bull serviced the cows on the prison farm and any other cow in the county that could make it to the farm. On monthly assigned breeding days they'd come, led by the farmer behind a mule and cart, or bawling and mooing on the back of a rickety pickup or on a trailer. The huge snorting bull, pawing and drooling, seemed to have a calendar in his head. He'd stand in the middle of the bull lot, small, red-rimmed blue eyes moist, flinging dust and dirt ten feet into the air, awaiting his next task.

Grandfather, Cap'n LL, allowed no jocularity as the bull did his duty for the county. He did not consider it a social occasion. He stood with the farmer and a trustee watching the breeding matter-of-factly until all the cows were serviced.

Since little was made of the breeding and no one ever tried to discourage my knowledge of the process, I was only remotely interested. I knew everything about it: The cow and the bull made a little calf inside of the cow and 66 days later it was born. The excitement didn't concern the making of the calf, much too small to be interesting. The excitement came at the birth of the calf, clean and precious and puppy-like.

I was quite young, no more than five, when I wandered alone down one of the white inmate wings. I stopped when I heard a ruckus, then a rhythmical whump-whumping from inside the hall closet. I pressed my face against the escutcheon. It was too dark to see through the keyhole, so I tried the knob. I had to pull hard, since that one was always bad to stick.

Giving it as much of a yank as a five year old can, I fell backward as it flew open. In the back, beside the long paper bags from the drycleaners full of winter clothing reeking of cleaning fluid, I saw Annie Mobley and a trustee. She was leaning forward with her skirt up over her back and her panties down. He stood behind her, really close, with his trousers around the tops of his brogans.

Always a child to drew on past experiences, I recognized immediately what they were doing. Moreover, they were not to be disturbed. Backing quietly outside and closing the door I skipped down the hall to the white folks' dining room where I saw Grandmother working on menus for the next day.

"Grandmother," I patted her arm until she looked at me. "Grandmother, Annie Mobley is going to have a calf!"

Grandmother's eyes were blank for moments behind the gold wire glasses with the half moons. I could see her pondering what I had told her. She reached into the cigarette pack-sized pocket on the bib of her apron to fish out her hearing aid, then thumbed the volume control and checked the earplug. "What, Becca?" she honked, holding the hearing aid closer to my mouth.

"A calf, Grandmother. Annie's going to have a calf." To underscore the message I finger-spelled "caf".

Grandmother lowered her face into her hand for a moment. When she looked up, her gaze was off in the distance, gathering herself. "My God," she breathed. "Becca," she whispered. She swept me close to her bosom. "What is going to happen to your mind, child?"

The maid working with her busied herself at the end of the table, looking away as if she had not heard my news. Aunt Martha was moving as quiet as a vapor toward the kitchen door.

"Martha," Grandmother honked, "Fetch Cap'n LL." Aunt Martha nodded and hurried to her task.

Grandmother plunked me in the chair she'd been sitting in. "Keep her right here," she honked to the maid. Clutching the back of her old-lady tricot skirt to pull it down over the tops of her stockings she launched herself across the dining room and through the big French doors leading to the lobby.

Aunt Martha and Grandfather appeared in what seemed like only a moment. Grandfather hadn't even bothered to take off his waders. Folded around his knees, they made him look as rakish as a pirate as he clumped through the kitchen to the inmate wing. I hopped off the chair to join him but he turned sternly toward me. "Stay there, girl," he said. I could tell he meant it. Five minutes later he returned, coming through the kitchen with the trustee walking, limber-jointed and jaunty, in front of him. Catching the maid's eye, the trustee made kissy noises to her. She dissolved in silent mirth, head down and shaking. Grandfather said nothing but swung one of his big gaiters, kicking the trustee on the seat of his pants through the swinging kitchen door.

Grandmother hated having trustees in the main house, but since a few chores required trustworthy, able-bodied young men, she settled for two out of the three attributes. The trustees were not in prison for nothing. Most of them had broken the law many times before they were ever incarcerated. "Trustee" was a relative term.

All the men between the ages of 17 and 40 who were worth a damn were in the service, creating a double-edged sword. On one hand the country missed their vitality and strength. On the other, the war years, when the men were gone, often seemed like a big pajama party for many of the women. Women took jobs they never dreamed they could do, adapting themselves to the workplace, cutting their hair, wearing new clothing. They spent their wages uncounseled by husbands, brothers or fathers. It was a heady experience for women in uncounted numbers.

My own aunt Elsie learned to drive the big 1939 Chrysler, the town's only taxi. Every day she drove to her office, a little glass-enclosed addition to the city hall built under the metal fire escape, about three times the size of a phone booth, but still with plenty of room for her desk and phone and a few other necessities. "Simpson Cabs," she'd answer the phone to find out where to pick up fares and where to take them. Much of her business went between Whitley's Hotel and the train depot, providing the basis for her business in more ways than one. Many of the recruits stayed over at Whitley's and needed to get down to the troop trains at a specific time. Those fares provided a very steady source of income.

More than that, Elsie, with an almost endless supply of gas ration coupons, was the most envied person in town. It was not uncommon for her to cram the cab full of folks and head for Norfolk. Often it was women going to meet troop ships full of husbands and sons.

Aunt Elsie was scrupulously honest about the fare to Norfolk, and made one thing very clear at the start of the journey: All luggage and duffel bags rode up on the luggage rack, no exceptions. The cavernous boot of the big Chrysler was where Elsie made her real profit. It was full of five-gallon demijohns of the best homemade liquor she could buy in the county. Sometimes her riders sat with demijohns between their legs. No one minded the crowded conditions and minor discomfort not only because of Elsie's fairness about the money, but also because after they crossed the Albemarle Sound bridge she would open some of her stock. By the time they arrived in Norfolk, everyone was glad to have made the trip.

Elsie had an instinct for business, supplying her contacts in Norfolk weekly and directing newcomers desiring feminine companionship to the proper sources. She made money on both sides of that transaction, getting fares and tips from the men she drove to the brothel, as well as a weekly stipend from the madam. The first nylon stockings in town belonged to Aunt Elsie. Their lines went up the back of her legs, disappearing into the folds of her short skirt. She loved the war years, having her own money and doing just what she wanted.

Other women found work at the pulp mill. Danziger hired any woman who wanted to work, not just in the office, but even on the line. They worked shiftwork, same as the men, and took their paychecks home the same way. Some went wild, single and married alike. With new clothes bought with their own money they loaded up in flivvers and headed for the dives near the Hertford Marine base to dance the night away.

They continued writing to beaux in places they had to search for on the map, writing as small as possible on paper so thin it hardly held up to folding. In return they received letters from boys they hardly remembered, full of cut-out areas and, if they were lucky, snapshots to pass around at work.

In contrast to the sentiments of popular songs of the time, mostly written by men, the women did not spend their time pining. They led full lives. For some it was the best of times.

The war years were good ones for Aunt Elsie and for me. After the war her economic success leveled off.

And my father came home.

Grandmother came back into the dining room with Annie, a crimson spot prominent on each cheek. They passed through the same swinging door into the kitchen as had Grandfather and the trustee. I hopped from my chair to look inside. Annie was getting the kitchen ladder from the closet. Dragging it over to the high pantry she started unloading it. It took her until early the next morning to wash every pot and every piece of glass and china in the big kitchen.

Later that summer Annie's seven year old daughter, Peggy, came to live with her. I was absolutely delighted. To me Peggy seemed like a goddess, unaccustomed as I was to other children. Her knowlege of the ways of the world astounded me. Within a week of her arrival I had learned to filch candy from Mr. Sexton's store across the big highway, had found hiding places in the barn, way up in the rafters that I had never dreamed were available to me, and went regularly down between the big crepe myrtle tree and the road to throw rocks at cars.

Our little-girl throwing arms, especially mine, were not what they could become with practice, so we hardly ever actually hit a car with a handful of gravel. Because of her age and increased experience, Peggy was better than I. She was grace itself, standing on the berm of the road, right hand hidden in the folds of her pinafore, full of pebbles. She would pretend to be walking along the highway, head down, and though she could not have identified the Doppler Effect by name, she surely did have practical knowlege of it.

When the sound of a car told her it was in just the right place, her arm would fly out, fingers flying open to deliver its payload of grill-scarring, paint-scraping, windshield-pinging rocks. Without waiting to see if we had connected, we fled up the little rise to crouch behind the big crepe myrtle, hearts pounding with exertion and excitement.

Many drivers would blow their horns when they saw our windup and delivery. On the few occasions when we actually hit a car, the driver would blow more than once and shake his fist at us. When my initial amazement wore off, I found myself exhilarated by the reactions of the drivers. I felt invisible to them, able to vanish behind the crepe myrtle.

That illusion was shattered one otherwise perfect day, when Annie Mobley had given Peggy and me pennies for candy at Mr. Sexton's store. With heads high and a little brown bag almost full, we headed over to the crepe myrtle to get in some rock-throwing. Popping a piece of Bazooka bubblegum into her mouth with one hand and flinging a rock with the other, Peggy connected. We scampered in our usual fashion toward the tree.

The horror that happened next seemed in slow motion. With a screech of brakes, the driver, gravel-stung, stopped his car, got out and ran toward us. Stunned, like fawns transfixed by headlights, we stood still long enough for the driver to get between us and the house. He grabbed us each by an arm and started shaking us, screaming about the unavailability of glass because of the war, the cost of new paint jobs, and how our parents would have to go to debtors' prison to pay for it all. In my stunned condition I started to offer that Peggy's mother was already IN debtors' prison, but Peggy glared at me and gave me a "Shut Up!" look.

Since Peggy was the older, he gave her an extra shake. "What is your name, little girl?" he demanded, spittle flying in his anger.

"Jane Green," Peggy answered, her eyes averted.

Her answer exploded in my brain. She was not only a goddess, she was an all-knowing one. Since she had shown me the way, I would follow her lead. I licked my little five-year-old lips in anticipation.

"And yours?" He shook my arm.

I dropped my eyes as she had. "Peggy Mobley," I answered. I looked to register her pleasure at my quickness in following her lead but instead found her thin-lipped and seething. Mystified and devastated by her anger, I hardly cared that the driver had spied my grandfather and was turning us in to the Law of Washington County.

Later Peggy tried to explain it, sometimes with words that would have gotten my mouth washed out, but my little brain couldn't fathom her anger. Finally, in disgust she settled for warning me never to say her name to anyone else. I didn't understand that, either, but to get back into her good graces, I agreed. Not until my brain was seven years old did I realize why Peggy was so mad at me.

Peggy was nine and Flo, her sister who was born to Annie instead of a calf, was three when Dr. Grey locked horns with Aunt Martha again. It was an occasion I never forgot. It started, as usual, with Peggy. Instead of walking straight home from school, she detoured through Rose's Dime Store, somehow adding three slender white candles to her possessions. She showed them to Flo and me, swearing us to secrecy. Quite a thinking person by then, I realized the implications of the oath-giving. Peggy had swiped those candles from Rose's and was hiding her booty.

She promised that we would all go out to our hideout behind the Ant Ocean, remove the crackling crisp cellophane from the candles, and light them. But until then she would hide them. I didn't see where she hid them, but Flo must have.

When I went down to the white inmate wing the next day, Flo was looking furtively into the closet. "C'mon," she whispered, pointing at the closet, her hand clutching the wooden matches. I gasped at sight of them and instinctively glanced down the hall. Grandmother could be upon you before you knew it when things like match-lighting were afoot.

Flo was standing in the closet, beckoning me. I shook my head and she closed the door smartly in disgust.

It took me a while to realize that there really was smoke coming from alongside the edges of the door. I tried to open it, but the doorknob burned my hands. I ran like the wind down the hall to the bathroom and dipped a towel in the commode. I knew I could handle the doorknob with that, but as much as I twisted and pulled, the door was stuck again.

I ran for Grandmother, screaming for her through the kitchen, finally, in dreamlike slowness, finding her in the black folks' dining room. When I reached her, my sobbing and panting were too loud to penetrate her hearing aid. She told me to spell. "Fire," my fingers flashed. "Fire in the white inmate wing."

"Martha," she honked. "Martha, call the fire department."

None of Aunt Martha's magic could conquer the technology of the telephone. She had never in her life even talked on one, and she stood like a statue. Grandmother flew into the kitchen.

"Annie. Get the fire department on the telephone. We have a fire in the white inmate wing." Annie flew down the hall to Grandmother's apartment. Aunt Martha, disgraced, ran behind Grandmother.

I could hear the sucking noise the fire was making as we got into the hall. I knew that Grandmother would try to get the door open and I signed to her that the knob was hot and showed her my hands. When she saw the blisters, she took my hands in hers, sobbing. "We've got to get the inmates out. You and Martha, understand? In the wheelchairs. All the way outside. Dump them on the lawn. Get the maids. Get all the wheelchairs. Do you understand, Becca? Get the ones in the back of the hall first."

I was the wind. I dumped Mrs. Peacock onto the lawn first. She probably could have made it walking, but she was very slow, and sometimes she had to have much explanation of the simplest things. Loading her up, I pushed her down the hall, across the lobby, out onto the porch and down the steps, tipping her onto the lawn under the live oak trees.

Mr. MacNerney was next. He could hardly stand by himself, and had to wear a rubber tube on himself. Then came Mr. Coy Brown who had had a stroke and could only remember swear words. Aunt Martha had gotten Miss Agnes Caughman, Miss Fairey Bell Belcher, and Burton Jackson. We passed the firemen going in with their hose and got Jessie Swain and James Ed Hassell, the final two on that hall.

The fireman shooed Grandmother back into the lobby. "When the fire hits that oiled floor, I don't know if we can hold it, Miz Bass," one of them told her.

"Martha, take Becca out under the live oak and keep her there."

"But Grandmother, I can get more people...."

Grandmother clutched Aunt Martha to her. "See to Becca, Martha. See to that child."

Aunt Martha and I sat in the grass watching the firemen run back and forth, listening to Mr. Coy Brown swear. She realized my hands were paining me and turned them palm up for examination. "I'm gonna blow out that fire, chile. I'm gonna blow out that fire now. Yo hans gonna be fine now. They gonna be smooth wif not a speck o' scar." She moved her hands over my upturned palms, not touching them at all, but breathing on them. I heard her chanting a poem over and over, something about angels coming from the East, bringing frost and taking fire.

Afterwards I felt no pain at all from the burn, though blistered flesh is hardly quickly forgotten. Even as I look at my palms today, there is not a sign of a burn anywhere on my hands. Maybe I was lucky not to remember the pain or to have ropey, puckered scars you sometimes see from burns.

Flo was not so lucky. The worst of it was that she didn't die immediately in the fire, but lived almost four days. The hospital was out of the question for Flo, ninety miles away by ferry and the sound bridge. She wouldn't have made it to the end of the driveway. Grandmother took rolls of bandages made from boiled cotton sheets and fixed Flo a little cot in the spare room in her apartment beside the double bed she gave Annie.

I didn't get to see Flo when the firemen took her out of that closet, but I heard one of them say that she was a mess, her hair, lips, ears and eyelids all burned off. He said she had inhaled the fire into her lungs. I just couldn't imagine what a person would look like with all those parts burnt off, so later that day I took my chalk and drew on the smooth cement of the porch how I thought the face would look.

Aunt Martha saw the portrait of the hairless, lipless, earless, lidless child and I could see it upset her. I thought it was because it was so grotesque. "It make her spirit linger here, chile, and it in 'nuf pain now. It need to go out dis house and off dis porch." With brushes and soap and water we scrubbed the porch until not a trace of the picture showed. Even so, it took Flo four days to die.

Annie sat by the window next to Flo's cot, her body sagging, her mouth open. Flo lay motionless, her face and arms bandaged under a tent of cotton sheeting. She couldn't eat or drink, of course, and there were only a few places on her body where Dr. Grey could put the big glass needle full of morphine.

For the four days she lived, all day and all night Flo made a grunting sound with each breath. I thought it was going to drive Aunt Martha mad. She had tried to get into Flo's room that first day to draw the fire out but only succeeded in enraging Dr. Grey. "Keep that bitch out of here," he ranted. "We're fighting infection all over that child's body, and she's lousy with germs and filth. We don't need more."

He actually seemed to think Flo could live like that. All Aunt Martha wanted was to help her with the pain, to allow her to die in peace. I knew it, and the adults, Dr. Grey included, did too. The battle lines were drawn, and Flo was caught in No Man's Land.

Late on the third night silence descended on the wing. All of us who lived on that wing were awakened by the absence of the sound that had had our nerves so much on edge. Flo was no longer making the little grunting sound.

Our initial relief was sweeping. We thought the absence of sound meant that she was dead and her suffering finished. Annie came into the hall where Grandmother stood with me, one of the maids, and Aunt Martha, Annie's eyes almost shiny with relief. "She's quietnin' down. I don't think it'll be long now." She nodded at Aunt Martha and squeezed her hand.

The rest of us went on back to bed, but Aunt Martha sat on a little hassock outside the room, whispering over and over the rhyme about the Angel from the East bringing frost and fire. She stayed out of the sick room, as per doctor's orders. That morning, just before Dr. Grey was due, the little girl died.

Annie had already picked out a coffin. It was waiting on draped saw horses in the lobby, looking like a little white trunk. I had looked inside before they put Flo in, and couldn't believe my eyes. Flo's coffin was a confection of white velvet and pink bows, not the gray flannel interior of most of the coffins that left the county home. Of those there were more than a few. Old sick people died.

I was more than a little puzzled by Flo's situation. Never in her short life had she or anyone she knew owned a dress that lovely. Now she would leave, in a party dress of a coffin, up the pasture to the poor peoples' graveyard to live 'til kingdom come behind strands of barbed wire keeping the stock out. I didn't understand it at all, but I knew better than to ask about it, just pondered it to myself.

The funeral took place quickly. Annie had no kin living near enough or caring enough to make the trip for a dead base-born child. Flo's father had been paroled before Flo could walk; after his initial interest in fathering the baby he had no thought of helping with her upkeep.

Though Annie was not a church member, the Missionary Society of the Free Will Baptist Church offered to have the service. Grandmother hesitated at the proposal, but agreed reluctantly.

The Missionary Society of the Free Will Baptist Church made one regular visit to the county home every week. On Wednesday the trustees loaded up the big fireplace with firewood and the maids moved the dining room chairs into the lobby to augment the sofas and upholstered chairs, turning them all to face the north end. Inmates unable to walk were rolled in on old-fashioned wheelchairs, lovely cousins of today's businesslike plastic and chrome ones.

The county home's wheelchairs were high-backed, made of golden oak, with woven cane in the seat and back. Two leg lifters operated independently of each other, and on some the oak and cane back could drop almost parallel with the floor. The large wheels had hard rubber tires and metal bracing to serve as brakes.

On Wednesday evenings the really old and non-ambulatory inmates were wheeled into the lobby and placed near the fire. They were always colder than the ones who could walk, who took seats in the dining room chairs or on the soft chairs.

Everyone in the Home looked forward to Wednesday. So did I, for two reasons: the Missionary Society always brought punch, and Mean Jimmy Speight and I almost always made some money on the evening.

James Arnold Speight — Mean Jimmy to all who knew him — had had infantile paralysis, just like Our President. The disease had withered one of his legs and had caused one of his arms to be held cocked and useless against his side. For all the world he looked like a plucked chicken wing. The March of Dimes Foundation had fitted him with a big silver brace that ran down inside his pants leg, coming together inside the heel of his funny-looking boot.

The silver brace didn't seem to do much for Jimmy's walking. He could make painful headway, but much of his energy was spent in the flapping motion of his arms and the effort of bracing his knees together to keep his body upright.

Nor did the brace do anything for his attitude, manners or ability to inspire affection in others with his silvered speech. Jimmy did not suffer the counsel of fools, alerting people to this attribute by an early warning system of name-calling and epithets. To Jimmy, the world was divided into two camps: Shitheels and Asswipes. Almost everyone fell into either of these two categories.

To help compensate for his leg and arm disability, Jimmy carried a cane, its staff tipped with a brass cap. In a pattern spiraling from the golden tip to the handle, the Bible verse from John 3:16 had been carved. The handle itself must have weighed three pounds; it was the carved head of Jesus, as big as a baseball and cast of solid brass.

Others with the same affliction and more disposed to chat might have used the cane as a way to start conversations, but not Jimmy. Sure, the cane was invaluable for ambulatory progress, but for Jimmy its main role was as an equalizer.

His idea of a warning was to swing the cane in a whistling low horizontal arch, cracking any shinbones within reach. When pressed, he'd bring the infernal machine over his head and down upon the offender, tip gleaming and staff making a satisfactory "thunk" on the noggin, raising goose eggs which often remained blue for the better part of two months, and often concealed a chipped bone.

The movement that made his name lore in our small town, however, was one requiring exquisite dexterity, finesse, and the utmost of hand-eye coordination. Jimmy was making his painfully slow way up the courthouse steps to appear before Judge Bateman. He'd been charged with using profanity in front of Barton Swain's wife, Myrla, after Barton had asked him to leave his store. Jimmy had replied that he had just bought a can of Tube Rose, and had every right to linger there to open his purchase.

When Barton told him to leave, Jimmy called him an Asswipe. He was winding up to name Myrla a Shitheel when Barton collared him and dragged him outside, setting him on a bench. Had Jimmy been able to get his can of snuff into his jacket pocket and give his cane proper attention, Barton would have been dead meat. Everyone who witnessed it knew that. Jimmy was about to pop a blood vessel.

Back inside, Barton was calling Grandfather's office to register a complaint. The call was taken by Deputy Joel Simpson, whom everyone called "Jo-el." Everyone wondered why Jo-el wasn't fighting in France with the rest of the boys his age. He looked strapping, taller than most, with a good head of light brown hair. Just like the men in boot camp, he did sit-ups and pushups every day, and even grey-haired women who had gone through the change were seen to fan themselves and cut their eyes when Jo-el passed.

What they didn't know was that with his 1-A body, Jo-el had 4-F feet. The Army doctor had taken one look at those feet and waved Jo-el out of the line. "We can't take anyone with talipes, son," he said.

"It ain't that bad, Doc. Look at this." Jo-el flexed his biceps. "And I can shoot, too. It ain't that bad, Doc." Jo-el was whining now. The doctor shook his head and waved Jo-el out of line. Humiliated, Jo-el returned home but kept his body in good shape in case the Army changed its mind. He took the deputy job so he could wear a uniform and have a gun. Just in case.

When Jo-el heard Barton's story, he wrote Jimmy a ticket for using profanity and told Jimmy he'd have to go before the judge. Jimmy made the air blue before Grandfather drove up and ordered him into the back seat of the car.

When Jimmy's day in court arrived, he left early, eschewing Grandfather's offer to drive him to the courthouse. He was halfway up those wide but low baby steps going up to the courthouse when Jo-el appeared on the marble stoop holding the courthouse bell on its metal stand. Jo-el watched Jimmy's progress for a few moments before giving the big iron wheel activating the bell a turn, then another. The bell pealed, announcing to the town that court was in session.

Most would have known not to smirk at a person working so hard yet making so little progress, but Jo-el was young and foolish.

Hiding his own bad foot, he skipped down those baby steps which were giving Jimmy so much trouble. "Lemme give you a hand there, Flap," he said.

Jimmy said not a word, bad or otherwise. Steadying one knee against the other, like a drum major he flipped the cane through the air in a golden flash, the three pound brass head of Jesus the size of a baseball gleaming like a comet as it arched through the air. He caught it by the bronze tip.

I saw the incident but I still cannot remember the sound that the bronze head of Jesus made as it met with the crotch of Joel Simpson's tight-fitting deputy pants he always kept ironed with knife-blade creases. The blow doubled him over at the waist, and though it puzzled me for years to come, every man in the courthouse square and on the steps and the sidewalk doubled over in a kind of sympathetic acknowledgement of Jo-el's receipt of the blow.

When the head of Jesus on the end of the cane hit him, Jo-el said, "Whoont!"

"Whoont!" said every man in the square and on the steps and sidewalk from their bent-over positions.

Mean Jimmy, who got his popular name that very day, was now the only man in sight standing upright. He twirled his terrible weapon through the air again, so fast that John 3:16 all but flew off, and caught it. He never even gave Jo-el a glance as he continued his labored progress up the steps.

Mean Jimmy never directed cuss words to me or to Grandmother, though he said them in our presence. Grandmother, though she heard them, chose not to react to them. I heard them, fascinated by the effect they had on others and the wonderful images they evoked, filing them away in my mind for later use.

Grandmother and I knew another secret about Jimmy. He was the only inmate at the county home without a roommate. No straight-living old person already in preparation for meeting his Maker would tolerate his presence for more than five minutes. Jimmy wouldn't allow the maids into his room, but kept it in such an immaculate condition it shamed all the housekeeping the women did in the rest of the Home. His secret was that he collected matches in his room. He didn't want the maids to tell on him.

On the few occasions when Jimmy went downtown he'd go into the bank and pick up one or two glossy matchbooks. He picked up more from the filling stations on the corner and glanced at the baskets holding his prize in the Water Street businesses. The office help, both men and women, would greet his visit with bated breath, watching as the twisted little man lurched through the door to pick up a matchbook or two. No one realized that Mean Jimmy was stockpiling matches.

When Grandmother realized that there was enough sulfur in Mean Jimmy's room to toast everyone in the County Home twice, she approached Jimmy with the idea of keeping them in the barn. Jimmy hit the ceiling but didn't cuss at her. Instead, for the first time in his life, he pleaded. Torn between Jimmy's odd collection and the need for safety, Grandmother compromised. Jimmy would have to keep his collection in metal cans. Jimmy could live with that. He began buying lard stands to fill with his matches.

She asked him one day about his curious collection. "When I die and go to hell, I want to be able to offer the devil a match for my fire, Miz LL," he told her.

"You aren't going to Hell, Jimmy," Grandmother honked. "There is no such place." Never had I heard anyone say anything like that before!

After Jimmy died of the flu, his weakened body unable to resist further, the trustees must have hauled twenty lard stands out of his room, along with a couple or three metal foot lockers.

Grandmother always took charge of getting the old people ready for the undertaker when they died. She sponged them down and put on some good-looking clothes. As she prepared Jimmy I saw her tuck a pack of matches in his inside jacket pocket.

The punch the Missionary Society of the Free Will Baptist Church brought was so sweet, one could feel the Islets of Langerhans popping off, annihilated, from one's pancreas. Two cups would bring on a diabetic coma. Three would make me so thirsty I would have Grandmother up all night bringing me water and taking me to the bathroom.

The punch was equal parts orange and pineapple juice with double that amount of Welch's grape juice. Grandmother let them use her big glass punch bowl with the little glass cups nestling around it like a covey of quail chicks. My child's mind knew that no one picked in higher cotton or cut on a fatter hog than we did when the Missionary Society came with punch. Never in my young life had I tasted such nectar. I loved it even more than the inmates and the maids.

Mr. Coy Brown, whose only speech since his stroke was cuss words, was always included on prayer meeting nights. After the second hymn he'd get warmed up, starting up as a buzz in the back of the room, sitting in his wheelchair. "Goddamn, goddamn, goddamn," he'd say, barely audibly. Everyone in the room had heard Mr. Coy before and knew what was coming. No one even gave it another thought.

The tempo of the singing and guitar strumming would pick up, two-part singing on "Send the Light," with basses and altos booming and the sopranos soaring. "Let it shine ("let it shine," boomed the basses) from shore to shore," trilled the sopranos. It was more excitement than Mr. Coy Brown could tolerate. Sucked by a vortex of exhilaration to join in with gusto, "Cocksucker, cocksucker, COCKSUCKER!" he bellowed happily. No one in the room even blinked.

He was quieter as we sang of fountains filled with blood but got cranked up and moved to expression as we sang "Will the Circle be Unbroken?", tears streaming down his face at "taking my mother to the grave." "Fuck!" sang Mr. Coy. "FUCK!" During the prayers, heartfelt as they were, Mr. Coy kept it down to a few mumbled "shits" and "cunts."

Before we knew it, it was time for punch and cookies. One of the members had used butter from her own cows' milk to make the cookies, so as not to use anyone's ration card except for the sugar. Wednesday was a truly splendid evening.

The money we made was more important to Mean Jimmy Speight than it was to me, but he had expenses that I didn't have.

When the brethren of the Missionary Society came into the

lobby after singing, Jimmy was all smiles. Hobbling over to the door on his withered legs, he welcomed the male members by showing them to seats on the sofas and chairs, making sure they sat in the deepest, softest sofa or a chair that engulfed them. If they rose to sing or to serve punch, Jimmy would give me a knowing look and hustle over to insist that they stay seated; they were honored guests, and besides, punch-serving was woman's work.

After the Missionary Society left, after the last of the inmates was back in the wards, and when the punch-sodden maids had drifted off to their rooms, Jimmy and I would remove the cushions from the upholstered furniture and look for change from the pockets of the men who had sat there. Jimmy taught me how to run my hands along the crevices and edges, gleaning the change we found there. We had to be swift. The window of opportunity was slight, and we were careful not to let anyone see what we were doing; the cut was small enough. Wednesday nights hardly ever netted us more than fifty cents each, but that was enough to keep me in Bazooka and Jimmy in Tube Rose until big-spending, guilt-ridden relatives visited on Sunday.

So the Missionary Society came for Flo's funeral. I was disappointed to find that there would be no punch, but Grandmother and the maids were preparing a special dinner for after the funeral. Tablecloths and napkins for the long tables were ironed. Knives and forks, plain in design but made of coin silver, were shining as much as their humble material allowed. Strands of tri-colored ivy from Grandmother's courtyard made little centerpieces for each table.

Grandmother's velvety purple May irises on stems drooling clear, viscous liquid stood in tall vases in the lobby near Flo's casket. Everyone had outdone themselves for the occasion. The floors were even newly cleaned and oiled. Mean Jimmy Speight looked hopefully at the men sitting on the upholstered furniture.

The preaching of the funeral started with song, much as at Wednesday night prayer meeting. The Missionary Society members had brought their guitars to accompany themselves in the lusty singing of the hymns. They sang "....oh, come angel band" that I thought was quite appropriate. They prayed, some standing, some on their knees, for the soul of little Flo.

The preacher rose. Life had been good to him, considering his humble birth and scanty education. His little church had a new red carpet up the center aisle and a new piano. His son was drafted before the sexual deviancy the family had known about for years could be revealed to the rest of the community. His daughters were still pre-nubile and docile.

Preacher Devereaux wore a navy blue wool suit with a pinstripe and a vest, off the rack from the stout men's section of Ganderson's store. He imagined the suit made him look like a banker. In fact, it made him look like a navy blue striped ice cream cone. The pants swept up from the tops of his shoes at a perfect cone-replicating angle. His massively rotund abdomen and chest were two scoops; the starched collar transformed his almost nonexistent neck, the wattles of his jowls and the rest of his face into a perfect spheroid. Since it was much too tight to allow for a healthy flow of blood, his head had the aspect of a cherry. The effect couldn't have been more perfect.

Instead of swaying from side to side as did the singers, Preacher Devereaux rocked back on his heels and up on his toes contrapunctually to the choir in hypnotic rhythm.

His preaching began with a prayer of disjointed phrases, references to biblical incidents I can only guess were familiar to everyone else in the room, as most nodded and voiced affirmation. Exhortations to the Deity merged into the body of the sermon as he began talking about the sinfulness of all flesh. Indeed, everyone in the room, Flo included, was sinful. His prime biblical touchstone seemed to be "The sins of the fathers are visited on the sons."

I saw Grandmother take her hearing aid from her pocket to thumb up the volume wheel. Something was afoot.

Preacher Devereaux became conspiratorial with the assemblage. "Of course, in this case, we know as we meet to sing and pray together that the sins of the mother...."

Grandmother was on her feet, clumping in her Dr. Scholls up to where the preacher stood. "Mr. Devereaux, if you would..." She gestured to the front door. Preacher Devereaux was stunned. Accustomed to being listened to, he couldn't believe the interruption. By a woman? During a funeral? By someone who wasn't a Free Will Baptist, or even a Baptist of any kind? Everyone else in the lobby was equally stunned. He followed her through the front door.

I looked for a sign from Aunt Martha that things would be all right, but she was going to keep out of white folks affairs, keeping her eyes down and her thoughts to herself. The maids were cutting their eyes back and forth at each other, and a trustee standing at the back was grinning. The inmates sat with their mouths open, but that was usual for most of them. The members of the Missionary Society were becoming anxious, whispering to each other.

Grandmother, who never realized how loud she was talking, could be heard honking, "I'm sorry, Devereaux, but the poor woman has suffered enough, and surely the child has, too. I cannot allow you to go on in this vein. You can close with a prayer, if you want to, but then you really have to leave. You are upsetting the inmates."

"This is the hand of the Lord, Miz Bass. The sinner never wants to listen to the word of God..."

"Mr. Devereaux, if you do not leave the premises right now I will send a trustee out back to get Captain LL and the guards to escort you." She was so upset her fingers were talking along with her voice.

"You are a cursed woman, Cornelia Bass. If you think you can get into heaven with Our Lord, you have another think coming." He was sweating with exertion, anger, and the choice of a wool suit on such a hot day in May. "As the Bible says, 'He who believes in Jesus has eternal life, and he who disobeys Jesus shall not see life — God's anger comes upon him.' He's talkin' about you, Miz Bass. God's anger will be on your head!" he almost screamed.

Without a word, Grandmother turned away and reentered the lobby into an expectant silence. The sun had moved close enough to its apex in the Southern sky to shine through the beveled panes running from top to bottom on either side of the front doors. A big blob of light, broken into its component colors, lay like an omen across Grandmother's blouse and neck and chin. "You are all welcome to join us for dinner after we bury little Flo," she said. That was the closest to a benediction Flo ever got.

Most of the Missionary Society members stayed after the burial for the meal. I was never sure why. Maybe they had just heard about Grandmother's cooking, and that there was always plenty on the table.

3

Besides the high drama of Flo's funeral and the continuing Wednesday night visits of the Missionary Society, my life was relatively religion-free for a Southern child. In second grade, before my father came home from the Pacific Theater (I found out later he didn't go there to see movies.) and things were freer, I did have one brush with ecumenism.

Barbara D'Autremont moved into Winesett Circle, along with Little Richwood the only areas of town with houses neither brick nor painted white. Indeed, they were pink and green and blue, birthday cake colors. Square and graceless, with thin facia boards, they had stingy little stoops instead of porches, and aluminum overhangs that looked like the eyeshade my uncle Calvin wore when he entertained the locals at cards.

Houses in Little Richwood and Winesett Circle were exactly alike, except for the paint and the house numbers, something else new in town. When the numbers went up, — actually painted on the houses, that is — people came to look. They all had indoor plumbing, which was not all that unusual. By that time all the houses in town did, except for the ones Dr. Grey owned up on Sugah Hill that rented by the week.

People in Little Richwood had moved to town when the mill expanded and all the trees in West Virginia had been cut down for pulp mills there. The Danziger Company, seeing the abundant water and ready transportation, both barge and rail, in eastern North Carolina, bought the property on the river and closed down operations in Richwood, West Virginia. The mill hands were told that jobs were waiting for them in the new location, if they wanted them.

Many of them moved. Jobs were hard to find there, even after the Depression, and families with anyone working were lucky. West Virginians with names like Cunningham and Tatum moved to town. Besides their strange, Irish and French-sounding names, strange foods — pretzels, for example — started to appear in the A&P. They wanted to know where to buy beer! They also seemed to think their squat little two bedroom pastel houses were great.

Winesett Circle was built to take care of the overflow from Little Richwood. The houses were much the same, except that they had three bedrooms. Mill foremen lived in Winesett Circle; even before International bought out Danziger and brought in the union, foremen could afford an extra bedroom.

Barbara moved into town with her foreman father in October of the school year. We all assumed she was from West Virginia, but that wasn't important. What shot through school was the information that she was Catholic!

Some parents talked darkly of moving their broods to the Wilbur school, fourteen miles down the road, to be away from the bad influences rampant in the town. Bad influences for them were West Virginians in their pastel houses with numbers, the new liquor store opening on Water Street, and Barbara D'Autremont, the Catholic.

Grandmother said the only people disgruntled about the changes were the old families who wanted both the money from the sale of the trashy land that Little Richwood was built on *and* the land itself, bootleggers with a stranglehold on liquor sales, and the Klan, always looking for someone new to hate.

Talking about the Klan in such a loud voice made me nervous. I had seen them twice, myself. They scared me to death both times. Grandmother honked that they were just a bunch of fat old assholes in sheets, but I hated it when she tempted fate by talking about them so loudly.

"That child probably has a bunch of metals around her neck," one of the maids said when she heard that a Catholic child was going to be in school.

Having cut my teeth on Prince Valiant in the funny paper, my heart thrilled. "Metals! And around her neck!" Would they be chain mail or a solid breastplate? "Surely not a breastplate," I thought. That would be too heavy for me, really strong for a girl my age. It would probably be lighter metal, like chain mail. Barbara was becoming more fascinating by the moment.

Only the men in Prince Valiant wore metal. The women wore wonderful gowns, with blond hair hanging in fat long plaits down their backs. The women rode horses occasionally but mainly stayed home and had blond twins while the men rode off to war. Prince Valiant had pretty much mirrored life in my hometown. But now we had the promise of the arrival of Barbara D'Autremont, coming with her metal.

"They worship idols, you know." The teacher I overheard was referring to Catholics. That was a new one on me. I had heard of idols from the Missionary Society so many times I guess I had taken them for granted. Idols and graven images. Baal. I'd heard of them, of course, but never really thought they'd ever have any impact in my own life.

I hurried to the library as quickly as I could and pulled a step stool over to the big dictionary on the oak lectern. It drove Mrs. Swain, the librarian, crazy when children used the big Webster's. She would hover around, looking over a child's shoulder to see that no dirty words like "womb" or "penis" were being researched.

"Here, honey, use the Little Golden Book of Words. Use the Collegiate. They've got all the words little children oughta know." She'd snap the big Webster's firmly closed before any dirty words could leap from the double columns and into a child's mind.

One day when I asked Grandmother about it she got that grim look in her eyes. When she went to her apartment she sat down at the little telephone table, thumbing up the volume wheel on her hearing aid while looking up a number in the phone book. Because of her deafness, Grandmother used the receiver in a different way. She put the earpiece over the hearing aid in the breast pocket of her apron and spoke into the mouthpiece that was now upside down. Certain the party called had as much trouble with the instrument as she did, she talked as loud as she could.

"Miz Swain? Cornelia Bass here," her voice so loud she could have probably called from the door and bypassed the phone completely. "Miz Swain, I want Becca to be able to use any book in the library she wants to use." She paused and listened as closely as she could. "Yes," she hooted. "Yes, even the big Webster's." "I will take responsibility for that, Miz Swain." "Yes. I will write a note to that effect." She hung up the phone without saying "Good-bye" like most people. The whole ordeal of using the phone was such a strain that she never did see it as an occasion for being sociable. Using the phone was serious business.

I flipped the big thin pages to "idol." By the time I had gotten the first definition Mrs. Swain was literally breathing down my neck. As it was late in the day the soda she had used for soaking her dentures the night before was letting go; her breath smelled like the inside of a boot. As much as I could ascertain, an idol was an object or thing — a "graven image" that was worshipped.

I fanned the fetid breath of Mrs. Swain and her store-bought teeth away with the cover of the big Webster's and took a deep breath. I paged through, looking for "graven image." There it was! "An idol made or carved of wood or stone or precious materials."

I hopped off the stool and out of the direct flow of Mrs. Swain's halitosis, stopping to think for a moment about what I had learned. Barbara D'Autremont, Catholic second grader in my very class wore metal and worshiped idols! She would surely move her idols with her to Winesett Circle.

What a splendid opportunity for me. Such excitement rarely came to our town. I made plans to befriend this Catholic child. I would make friends with her and gain her confidence, then enter her home and see her idols. I could hardly sleep at night for the little thrills of anticipation and danger I felt from my plans.

At ten o'clock on an October Tuesday Barbara D'Autremont came to our school. We looked up to see the door of our classroom open, and Mrs. Cooper, the elementary principal, come in with a little girl and her mother. "Children, I'd like for you to say hello to Barbara and Mrs. D'Autremont."

"Hello, Barbara. Hello, Mrs. D'Autremont," we chorused. I felt as if electricity were coursing through my body.

She was not wearing her metal. I must have been silly to think she'd wear it to school. It was probably enough of a burden being Catholic without calling more attention to oneself by wearing chain mail. But I was really disappointed. I looked around at my compatriots. They didn't seem to understand the importance of what was happening in our classroom, or if they did, they cared not one whit.

Mrs. D'Autremont seemed normal enough. Her clothing was not out of the ordinary, either, a simple sweater set with no metal in sight. I wondered momentarily if she were Catholic; I hadn't heard anyone say, but I reckoned it was probably hereditary, or something, like the hemophilia in Dr. Grey's family. Of course she was Catholic. She probably had her own metal, but adult woman-sized. She probably had her own idols, too. I promised myself to find out by the end of the week. In my mind's eye I could see a whole section of Barbara D'Autremont's house in Winesett Circle devoted to idols and the storage of armor.

Those of us who had finished our work were allowed to draw until first recess, so I had time to think about Barbara's house. My mind played back to the definition of idol in the big Webster's. I distinctly remember the use of "worship." What did that mean, exactly? The Missionary Society, of course, had uttered it often, but I had never really thought about its meaning. I remembered an incident from my earlier life, flicking my mind across it to see if anything I had learned then could be of help in understanding this little brown-haired girl, new to our class.

It had happened in July, just after my birthday, with the tobacco in the fields tall and full of sap. July was a terror of a month for tobacco farmers. Every natural force in the universe seemed to take a whack at the weed, and every whim of an uncaring world could harm it.

The pride of the Coastal Plain was the big golden leaf. It had to be top quality to fetch top money. If a farmer turned his back for just a minute and missed the hornworms, they'd hatch out, leaving his leaves to look like Swiss cheese, hardly worth the money for the wood to cure the crop.

The old sotweed had been hybridized to get the most leaf out of every plant. The big light green leaves turning to jockey for position in the Carolina sun were unnaturally large for the strength of the stalk. Like a rich man's sloop carrying too much sail and not enough ballast, the slightest wind could knock it down. And July was the month of squalls and hurricanes. Squalls were bad enough, with lightning walking through the sky incinerating tobacco barns and killing both farmhands and livestock. The hail that often accompanied the squalls would cut a field to ribbons in an instant.

Looking across the pasture south of the County Home over by the graveyard, I could hardly believe it when I saw trucks there. As I watched, men began unloading large amorphous bundles that must have been heavy, it took so many to handle them. They pulled and strained and heaved, and before my wondering eyes, a circus tent began to rise.

I thundered through the halls to find Grandmother to tell her the news. When I did, I questioned for the first time in my life whether she really loved me. "It's not a circus, Becca. It's a church." She cast around for a way to explain it to me, but I took it as an out-and-out fabrication.

I knew perfectly well what a church looks like. The big Baptist Church on the corner of Fillmore and Fifth was built of red bricks, with a regular cliff of cement steps leading up to the big front doors. On the side of the church facing the main street was a big round window with a bleeding Christ hanging on a cross that you could really see best at night with light shining through it. It surely didn't have a pole holding up the middle of the thing!

Surely this was a ruse, an excuse to not take me to the circus, even though it was practically in our own yard. Who could understand the minds of adults? Even the sane ones like my grandmother and grandfather seemed prone to great waves of fever and destruction when really important things were concerned.

My experience told my young mind that I could allow her to become really impacted on this circus thing, or I could take matters into my own hands when the situation cooled down. I chose the latter. Instead of crying and raising cain, thereby running the risk of being banished to my room without any possibility of getting to go to the circus, I would be the very model of decorum. I simply nodded, accepting without words her circus lie, going off to play without whining.

All afternoon I sat on a little grassy hillock down by the end of the Home. If anyone asked, I told them I was looking for four-leaf clovers. And I did. Whenever I heard anyone on the porch above or on the driveway, I caressed the grass and clover to the side with my hands, parting the blades and stems to look for the green anomalies that would bring good fortune. In reality I watched the circus tent go up.

The men unfolded the whole tent and spread it into a big circle. Using the big flatbed truck they pulled up the center pole. I was too much the neophyte to wonder why elephants were not doing this job, or indeed to wonder where the elephants were.

To those jaded by the passing of many circuses the tent would have seemed a faded, poor excuse for canvas, but I didn't care that it was patched. I could hardly believe it when the side walls of the tent were rolled up and tied. Folding seats, wooden and grouped in fours, were set up in rows inside. I could see other equipment being moved about; my imagination went wild.

Knowing I should have something to show for my afternoon's work on the hill, I plucked two leaves from a clover leaf group, sticking it with a little blob of spittle and dirt onto the stem of a regular clover with similar sized leaves. If it flashed past Grandmother's eyes quickly, perhaps she wouldn't notice the alteration.

After serving supper to the inmates Grandmother often went out to sit and relax in the Adirondacks under the big live oaks before eating her own supper. On the days my little girl belly could wait, I would eat with her.

"Did you find a four-leaf clover?" she signed. Reaching into the pocket of my pinafore I gently fished out my creation, holding it just so by the fake adobe on the stem. "Oh," she honked and touched the leaf which promptly fell off.

She swept me into her big soft bosom, laughing her one-note hollow laugh. "Are you trying to fool me, Becca?" she honked. She was omnipotent, proof that when one sense is diminished the others became more acute. The woman saw everything. She knew everything I did, my every thought. I signed and leaned into her, exhausted by the heat and excitement of the day. We had supper in her little courtyard after I had my bath. I sat with her at the little picnic table, trying to stay awake.

A little yawn lifted her shoulders. My life brightened. "You need a nap, Grandmother," my fingers told her. I yawned because Mean Jimmy had taught me long ago that another person can hardly keep from yawning when some one else does. Sure enough, she yawned again. "No, I'm going to read first. But it is time for you to go to bed, Miss Prissy." She expected resistance from me but got none. I already had on the pajamas made of the nylon my father had sent from the war. "Made from a parachute," Grandmother had told me and showed me a picture.

I lay in my bed in a shaft of light from Grandmother's lamp, watching her slowly turn the pages of the Progressive Farmer. If she started reading the recipes or started changing them from the published servings of eight or ten to the fifty to eighty people she served each day, all would be lost. She would never nap.

Feeling myself slipping into the oblivion of sleep, I crept out of bed and sat beside the door, watching her. She nodded and her head jerked. Rubbing her eyes under her glasses she tried to read again. Slowly her head lay back on the antimacassar. The magazine slid from her lap, toward her knee, then fluttered down beside her shoe.

I froze, watching carefully. If she was going to wake up, it would be now. A little snore puffed out her cheeks, making her lips say, "Phfffft!" Quiet as moonlight in the hall, I slid out onto her porch and down the steps. Keeping close to the shubbery I crossed the lawn. Ordinarily I would have worried about snakes biting my bare toes, but tonight my feet had wings. I crossed the gravel driveway, headed for the fence that kept the cows in the North pasture. The tent was lit. People were going in. Not a moment was to be lost.

I paused momentarily to unsnag my pajama bottoms from the barbed wire, thankful my flesh was not involved. All southern children know that lockjaw comes from barbed wire and from stepping on rusty nails. We knew all the tales, how afflicted youngsters, jaw muscles clenched tight as a fist, would starve to death. As I skipped along avoiding cowpies, it occurred to me to wonder whether money would be involved in my circus venture. Crouching behind the wheel of the flatbed truck, I saw the sides of the tent still rolled up. There would probably be no admission charge! I waited there to see how it would begin.

Lots of people were coming to the circus, of all ages, really, but to my surprise more adults than children. They parked their old flivvers and pickups as close to the tent as possible. Even though it was dusk, the day had been hot, muggy, and dusty; no one wanted to walk far.

Sure enough, there was no admission. People walked right in to the tent from all directions, taking seats on the wooden folding chairs, four to the section. The back rows filled up first, which also seemed strange for a circus. I would have surely wanted to be up front so I could see.

The seats filled up and we all waited for the circus to begin. Nothing was happening outside the tent, so I crept closer, standing just outside the shadow cast by the oil lamps lining the inside of the tent. Everyone was looking to the back of the tent, waiting as I was.

A man in a regular-enough-looking suit came to stand in front of a cross made of wood with the bark still on it. To my surprise, the audience started singing songs, the same songs the people from the Missionary Society sang. Hearing recognizable music made me feel more comfortable, so I crept inside and sat on a crate under one of the lanterns.

After a few more songs, the man in front of the cross with bark on it began to talk about how it was going to be at the time of the end of the world. I was aghast. It was the first I'd heard that that was going to happen. Did it have anything to do with the war effort? Maybe another bond drive would avert such a disaster.

As the man spoke of a world of sinners, his helpers went along the edges of the tent, turning off the lanterns. Everyone in the tent gasped and blinked as a blinding light shot from the back of the tent illuminating the white screen where the man had been standing.

It seemed like magic when the first images appeared on the screen, a pictorial representation of sinners all over the earth. These were not movies, like down at the Town Theatre. These were still shots, actual photopraphs. Those sinners in the pictures would have never been allowed to continue to further action, not by the assemblage in that tent. What was presented to us on screen was scandalous.

Sinner women, cigarettes in one hand and beers in the other, were dancing with men who, from the looks of them, were just the right age for the army. Other sinner women with low-cut tight-fitting blouses barely concealing breasts that seemed to have a life of their own, requiring not one bit of support to keep them at such an acute angle, were luring soldier boys and other clean-living types away from happy homes filled with frowsy faithful wives and hordes of drippy-nosed children.

Men were pictured sitting in barber shops leering at magazines not shown to the audience. What we could see were unfinished chores in the yards of these men. "Sloth," thundered the man in the suit. "Sloth and lechery."

Sinners sinned on the mountains, beside the sea, and on the plains. The Deity was not fooled, however. He had big plans for them all during the ending of the earth, and this man was going to explain it to us.

He showed us pictures of the End of the World, far beyond any pictures of war damage I had seen. Mountains exploded into fiery jelly flowing and surging over sinners living on the heights. Even though the pictures didn't move, the simplest of us could see the agony of those mountain sinners, so vividly portrayed in slide after slide until every one of them was covered in molten gelatinous lava. Not a house or tree or even one person was spared who stayed there.

A few of the more clever mountain sinners tried fleeing to the sea to avoid the fire in the hills, but alas, the seaside sinners had their hands full. The sands beside the sea smoldered and the sea itself became an immense boiling cauldron. Fish and whales and sailors on ships alike were parboiled. I peeked at the carnage through fingers of my own hands covering my eyes. The end of the world was far worse than I even dreamed it would be when the man first brought it up.

But there was more. The Almighty had something special in store for the sinners who lived on the plains. The plains sinners continued with their wicked ways, considering themselves far enough from the fire-belching mountains and the boiling ocean not to worry. Then it appeared, created by the all-just God for the plains sinners: a huge metal contraption looking like a ten-story sand spur. The body of the thing was a sphere. Protuding from it were slender but sturdy spikes, sharper than mere humans could ever have made. The horror of it was that it could move on its own, sensing the presence of the plains sinners no matter where they hid.

We were shown a picture of the infernal plains-sinner contraption first sans sinners. Then in a scene that would become a Petrie dish for nightmares in the future, the Deity cranked up the sinner-sticker. The reaction of the plains-sinners was the same as mine, frightened to the point of immobility. They stood, dumb as I, watching in horror as the thing simply rolled over them, impaling them like so many olives on cocktail picks, packing their bodies twenty to fifty deep on each spike, cleaning out the sinners on the plains.

Before the man at the projector could show the next slide, I managed to find my legs. Bolting from the tent, I ran crouched through the maze of old cars and trucks, trying to get my bearings and find the direction to home. Beyond where the cars were parked, the long grasses and tussocks of the pasture tripped me up, but as well as I could tell, I avoided the omnipresent cowpies.

I ran toward the lights from the big lobby, flailing against the cruel barbs of the fence before I knew it. I sobbed once as I briefly confused the fence with the sharp spikes of the horrid contraption that impaled the plains sinners, then sobbed again in relief when I realized it was just the fence. The worst I could get was lockjaw, and I would at least have a few days to say a tearful goodbye to my grandmother.

My bare feet flew back across the sharp gravel of the driveway, feeling every edge, yet knowing that each step took me closer to the security of my own surroundings. Every step took me closer to Grandmother and Aunt Martha. When I got to the lawn I headed for the edge near the shrubbery, not even caring that the toe-eating snakes were probably out, waiting for me. I sped along to the porch leading to Grandmother's living room and burst through the door.

Grandmother and Aunt Martha were sitting on the big striped sofa waiting for me. Tears had been flowing down my cheeks since I got caught in the fence, but now they seemed to squirt from my eyes. I caught a bloody toe under the edge of the rug and sprawled, almost hitting the coffee table. I was on my feet in a split second, flying through the air toward both of the women on the sofa.

I clung there with an arm around each woman's neck, my skinny little pajama-clad body wracked with terror and sobs. They rocked me, holding me until I almost drifted into a fitful sleep. My grandmother said in a voice she thought was gentle, "Martha, draw a tub of water. We have to see to these cuts."

I heard, and knew immediately that there was more pain to come. I would have to brave the dreaded Merthiolate to have a chance at life. Grandmother was not doing this to punish me for my wanderings. She was on a mission to kill the awful germs swarming into my cut and bleeding body with the most powerful ammunition in her arsenal.

I had heard that some women, in their fight against disease, used iodine, which stung and left a yellow stain. Others used the pink-staining Mercurochrome that dripped in prissy droplets from a spatulate glass applicator attached to the rubber stopper. Since it didn't sting, it was certain to leave disease to breed and flourish in children sadly unloved by their parents.

Aunt Martha stripped off the nylon parachute pajamas my father had sent me, wet almost to the knee from dew and picked once at the seat of the pants and several times on the back. In a few places where the barbs had caught, runners extended up and down the fabric in little ladders. Aunt Martha bathed me in the big tub in Grandmother's bathroom. She washed my long thick hair with lots of shampoo, lathering me twice. I knew better than to cry and whine when soap stung my eyes and the cuts on my back and feet. I knew that Merthiolate was yet to come.

If iodine stained the skin yellow and stung a little, Merthiolate was neon orange and unmitigated liquid hell. Grandmother kept the bottle with the little black screw on top in her medicine chest. In her doctoring, she would open the cut with her fingers and tap droplets of the medicine into the wound. A mere cut would be covered with a Band-Aid, but a puncture wound would remain unbandaged. She said punctures needed to breathe.

I know she applied the Merthiolate, but I cannot remember it. What I do remember is waking up screaming in my grandmother's bed that night, but not because of my injuries which were minor.

Later that summer, when my cousin Gordon was visiting, we were crouched beside the driveway trying to coax a doodle bug out of his hole with a little knot of saliva mixed with dirt on the end of a straw. I became conscious of something very large close to me, perhaps a shadow moving across the yard or something. I looked up to see bearing down on us a silver orb the size of half the sky. Screaming, I rolled under the green Chevy Uncle Milton had bought before the war.

One part of my mind knew exactly what it was: a dirigible from the factory in Elizabeth City. We'd stopped by the factory with its mountainous hangars many times on the way down to the cottage at Nags Head, and had seen a hundred dirigibles. But for a moment it resembled the infernal machine coming to collect us all on spikes for delivery at the end of the world.

I walked up to Barbara D'Autremont on the playground and offered the absolute ultimate exchange of knowledge one second grade girl can give another. "I'll show you where the girl's bathroom is," I told her. Her countenance glowed with appreciation. I knew I had her.

Before the month was over she had asked me to her house after school to listen to Big John and Sparky on the radio. Though my body was almost vibrating with anticipation, I was ever so careful not to raise any suspicion. Sitting in my hideout behind the big wingbacked chair sitting catty-wampus across the corner of the room, I pondered how to maneuver Grandmother into letting me go. I finally decided that being straightforward and truthful would be best. "Grandmother, I want to go over to Barbara's house and listen to Big John and Sparky tomorrow after school."

"That's fine, Becca. Write down Barbara's phone number for me and be home before dark." She hardly looked up from the Progressive Farmer. I could hardly contain myself. I thought tomorrow would never arrive.

Barbara's radio was not a floor model like grandmother's but sat on a table in the living room, a little dark brown rounded-off box looking more like a loaf of bread than a radio. But I wasn't there to facilitate radio programs. I was there to see idols.

I wondered for a moment if Barbara's mother would serve us beer and pretzels, neither of which I had ever seen, much less eaten. Even though she was from West Virginia, she served us hot chocolate and store-bought cookies, just like any mother.

Hoping the ordinary snacks were not a portent of things to come, I glanced around the living room furtively. Mrs. D'Autremont must have seen my glancing; she took me over to the hall and pointed to the bathroom, inviting me to use it whenever I wanted. I got a good look at the hall and the location of the three bedrooms. There were no idols in the hall.

I ate another cookie, listening with half an ear to Big John and Sparky reading off a list of children with birthdays. Sure that Mrs. D'Autremont was busy with her meatloaf and Barbara was listening to the program, I boldly crossed the living room and into the hall.

I hadn't been wrong. There was not a trace of an idol in the hall, nor were there idols in the bathroom, either. I didn't really have to go, so I waited a minute and then flushed. I ran the water in the sink to let Mrs. D'Autremont know, if she were listening, that little non-Catholic children washed their hands. As quickly as I could, I glanced into each of the bedrooms on my way back to the living room but couldn't linger enough to see if any of them housed the idols.

Sparky had just read the last of the birthday names as I returned. "Barbara, let's go to your room," I suggested.

She made a face and took another cookie. "Big John and Sparky isn't over yet," she whined. I sat down, trying to exhibit more patience than I felt, but my restlessness was showing.

Mrs. D'Autremont looked up from meatloaf mixing twice and caught me squirming. "Is there anything wrong, dear?" she asked in that funny West Virginia nasal twang. West Virginians always sounded like they were going to sing a song about Mama.

"No ma'm."

"If you have to go to the bathroom again, feel free."

My God, it was like a gift. I couldn't believe my luck. "Thank you, Miz D'Autremont." I hopped up and darted toward the hall. The first bedroom was small. The yellow checked bedspread and the dolls on the pillow told me it was Barbara's room. There was no idol in the room or in the closet. The next room had an adult-sized bed and a regular dresser and chest of drawers just like any bedroom. Again, no idol there or in the closet.

I crossed the hall to the third bedroom, my heart hammering against my ribs. This room was darker than the other two, making me strain to see into the shadows. Next to an old treadle sewing machine sat an Electrolux on its little sled just like my grandmother's. When I turned to check out the closet I saw it. The idol was right beside the closet door!

I took a deep breath, trying not to panic. "Should I worship?" I asked myself, but couldn't think how. Should I touch it or would that offend it, make it mad? It might have some magical power to hurt me.

The bedroom door swung open and the door knob hit me on the

shoulder blade. I yelped in pain and terror, thinking at first it was the idol, but it was Barbara and her mother. "What's the matter, honey? Couldn't you find the bathroom?" I mentally checked the crotch of my panties, thinking maybe she knew something I didn't.

I could see she was uncomfortable that I was in the room. "I wasn't going to touch it," I assured her.

"Touch what, honey?" She switched on the light and looked around the room.

"Your idol, ma'am." I always 'fessed up when angry adults were closing in.

"My idol?" I nodded toward where it stood beside the closet door.

"I declare, you young'uns are so strange sometimes. This is a dressmaker's mannequin, not an idol." She took the piece of cloth off it and showed me how it could be adjusted to different sizes.

Still rooted in place beside the door, I knew I had to leave before she started asking me any questions. "I have to go now, Mrs. D'Autremont," I turned and was into the hall in a flash.

"Big John is still on," Barbara whined.

"I have to go now, Barbara."

"You're home early," my grandmother said. "Is Barbara a nice girl?"

"She's just a regular old person," I replied. She didn't even have any idols and no metals, either, from what I could see. I was nice enough to her after that, even though I had been disappointed. But we were never very good friends.

4

The time before the war ended, before my father came home, was good for me. It was like being Anne of Green Gables but with a twist.

Even the deadening effect of school didn't dampen my spirits. My mother happened to be home for the first day of school and she took me. My curiosity about school more than made up for my lack of curiosity about my mother, who was not much more than a stranger, an interloper in my young life. My mother had gone off to be close to her sailor husband. It wasn't all that uncommmon; there was even a word for it in the area: seagulling. What was uncommon was leaving children behind to be cared for by others.

We rode uptown in my Aunt Elsie's taxi, stopping at the 421 Diner for a grilled cheese sandwich which the cook put in a little white bag, folding the flap over. She put the bagged sandwich in another larger white bag, along with a strange wooden implement looking like a spoon with teeth, and a paper napkin. Even in two bags the sandwich was so greasy that by lunch time at school translucent circles appeared on the bag. The sandwich was cold, of course, but the spoon-fork made up for it.

I sat there most of the day in my new dress and my socks with the crocheted tops waiting for something to happen and learned the first lesson of school. School is where you wait most of the day for something to happen.

There were books everywhere in the room in long low red bookcases. Not one child made an attempt to get one of them, and I didn't want to be the one to set the precedent. I just waited.

Mother had left on the train again, so Grandfather drove me to school the second day. When we drove up to the school I wanted to blow the siren, which he sometimes let me do, but he said it wouldn't be appropriate — whatever that meant — in front of the school. I told him the the other children would be just thrilled. He usually loved it when I used the word "thrilled," but today he wouldn't relent, so I went to join the screaming mass of children in front of the schoolhouse door.

I hadn't known there were that many children in the world! I knew Peggy and my cousin Gordon and Billy Coburn who lived down the street. Never in my wildest dreams did I think there were so many children. They screamed and ran, working like maggots in the school yard.

Billy Coburn was five years old and not in school yet, but he was already bigger than Peggy who was three years older. He was such a mean little boy and had achieved such a reputation in his five short years that adults would not let him play with their children. Grandmother said that we should give Billy a chance but changed her mind after seeing him at play one afternoon.

Billy had unfastened one of the chains from his swingset and was swinging it in a whining circle while chasing Peggy and me. Before she could get out to the yard to stop him he had gotten me across the thigh, breaking the skin and tearing my pinafore, and had hit Peggy dreadfully close to her eye. One of the links, as it whipped around and hit the back of her head, had pulled out a tuft of her dark brown hair.

Billy spat and kicked at Grandmother as she held him while we ran for Grandfather. It took Grandfather and a trustee to get Billy home. Aunt Martha said that Billy needed his butt cut.

One afternoon as Billy wandered down the street, he saw Peggy and Gordon and me jumping rope. Five minutes later he was throwing dirt clods at us. The three of us decided we had had enough of Billy and were able to get him on the ground and tie him up with our jump rope. Gordon and Peggy held him down while I ran inside to get an extension cord.

We stood him on his feet and dragged him, screaming, over to a big light pole with a guy wire. It took some doing; Billy could really kick. We finally managed to get him tied to the guy wire. I wrapped the extension cord around him a few times and tried to pry his mouth open to put the end inside, but he wouldn't open his mouth. Instead, I tucked the end under his arm, prying the prongs apart to stick the guy wire between them. "Billy," I told him, "when the street lights come on downtown, you're going to be 'lectrocuted."

Billy could see as plain as the rest of us the gathering darkness, and lights starting to come on three blocks away in the windows of Barton Swain's store. His screams increased in volume as the row of street lights began to flicker on.

Before we had a chance to see if we could fry Billy, Grandfather was behind us. "I told this young man never to come here again," he said gruffly. We all stood aside, hardly daring to breathe as Grandfather untied Billy. Billy's screaming had tired him so that he could hardly stand. He steadied himself against the guy wire long enough to launch a big wad of spittle toward Grandfather and then ran as fast as he could toward home.

Grandfather coiled the extension cord and passed it to me. "Next time he comes down here we'll have to see if your idea works, Becca." We walked hand-in-hand back to the County Home.

Billy did indeed come back. Discovering him up in my hideout in the big crepe myrtle tree, anger at his defilement of my place surged through me. He had found the Tube Rose can with the Blue Diamond single-edged razor blade in it.

The Blue Diamond was pure contraband, an article about which children did not even aspire to or ask about because of the effect it had upon adults. Grandmother kept the blades way up in her medicine chest shelf, past where I could reach even if I stood on the basin. One day she had a fit when, out of the corner of her eye, she saw me reach for the little cardboard band that sheathed the sharp edge of the blade.

"No, no, no," she honked, spelling with both hands. "You are never to touch that. You could cut a vein and bleed to death, Becca!" She swept me into her big soft bosom and almost hugged the wind out of me. I could hardly believe how much the possibility of my bleeding to death had affected her.

Grandmother used the Blue Diamond in conjunction with a fifteen-inch-long pair of blue-black shears kept sharp by a family of gypsies who passed through the area two or three times a year.

The gypsies rode in a bright wagon with symbols painted on the side: stars, footed cups, sticks and swords on one side, the side I liked best. On the other were pictures of strange people, some dressed like Prince Valiant people and others like scary skeletons or people hanging from ropes. I hated that side of the wagon and wouldn't look at it because it gave me nightmares.

When they came to grind the knives to an incredible edge and patch the holes in the pots and pans, they also sharpened all the scissors in the house. Since it was an all-day job, they camped overnight in the field behind the poor folks' graveyard, over near the woods. Grandmother always invited the wife of the knife grinder to come for water. When she came, Grandmother would have two chickens, tied by their legs and lying on their sides, beside a peck basket. Inside were eggs and vegetables, a big block of butter and some cold biscuits. The dark woman would smile and nod her thanks, and offer to read the Tarot cards for Grandmother.

Grandmother would always thank her, pretending she had enormous amounts of work to do, and the gypsy woman would walk back to her wheeled home, so graceful and dignified to my admiring eyes.

Grandmother would hurrumph about Tarot cards. Until the gypsies left she kept me close to her side. With her tools sharp and her pots mended she was ready to face the monumental task she and only she did with the old people. After the maids had finished bathing them, Grandmother would enter their rooms with an enamel basin of warm water, her pack of Blue Diamonds and her shears, along with a towel and a big bottle of Jergens lotion. Pulling a chair to the side of the bed, she turned the supplicant's body so that the legs were hanging over the side to soak in the basin.

While the feet were soaking, Grandmother and the maid stroked the lotion onto the old person's arms and body. A delicious smell of cherries and almonds permeated the room. When the inmate's feet were ready, Grandmother would dry them with the towel, then cut the nails on that foot with her big blue-black shears. Her hands were sure and steady, cutting the nails just so, straight across, short enough not to snag sheets and socks, but not so short the nail could become ingrown and painful. She could cut so that the trimmings didn't go zinging off into space but remained on the growing nail by a tiny tag. With the ease of cutting a thread with those fearsome-looking shears, she'd nip the piece and deposit the trimmings in the trash can.

She filed the cut edges of each nail with her long metal nail file rounded to an almond-shaped point on one end, which set some of the recipients' teeth on edge. But they endured it, loving the special attention they so seldom received. Next, Grandmother took a new Blue Diamond and unwrapped it. Discarding the cardboard band she went to work on the softened callouses on the old people's feet. Ever so careful, she honed them with the blade, then smoothed them with a piece of pumice.

After shaking some Jergens into her hand and warming it to the temperature of her own body, she massaged it into the old person's feet. She took her time, giving attention to heels and insteps and to each toe. The inmates would be practically purring by the time she finished, at least those who were still awake.

Grandmother administered to the white inmates first and then the black ones on the back wing. She took the same care with each foot of each person, cutting the nails, smoothing the callouses, checking for fungus and gangrene, smoothing on the lotion.

Crazy Joe was the only one who hated getting his feet tended to. Since he stayed in the woods most days, Grandmother would wait for him out back at dusk with her foot-tending equipment, a plate of hot biscuits, and a glass of sugary tea with a big wedge of lemon. Then the drama would begin.

Crazy Joe loved fig preserves. When he emerged from the

woods, there would be Grandmother, putting a fig on a biscuit half and drizzling some of the syrup onto the bread. Pointing to the step on which she wanted him to sit, she waited. The old black man would grimace, gnashing his teeth and pulling at his wild hair.

Grandmother had the patience of Job. Finally he'd sit on the step. She'd give him the fig biscuit, and the process would begin. Into the tub of warm water went his feet, brown on top and pink on the bottom. While she waited for his toenails to soften she sat on the step behind him, gently combing the twigs and grass from his hair. With silver scissors and gentle hands she trimmed his hair and beard, stopping only to give him another fig biscuit. Then, as dusk deepened, she sat beside him for a while, sometimes with her arm around him.

A person's toenails and fingernails can grow amazingly when left alone. By the time Grandmother got to him once or twice a year, Crazy Joe's looked like claws. She really had to bear down on those big blue-black shears to cut those toenails, but she always managed. She also examined the pink part of his foot carefully but didn't cut his callouses; since he never wore shoes, summer or winter, Joe needed them. She dried his feet and got out the Jergens. Joe loved that part.

One day after Grandmother had tended to Miss Fairey Bell Belcher's feet she forgot to put the Blue Diamond into the trash can and left it on the table beside her bed. I started to draw her attention to it but kept my mouth shut and waited. Later that afternoon, I went back. It was still there.

Miss Fairey Bell was a very old woman, small and drawn in on herself, her skin so thin her veins stood out like cords. Her whispy white hair, as fine as a child's when she was a young woman, now seemed more like a puff of smoke or a wisp of vapor. Her white round scalp looked for all the world like a cue ball if it hadn't been for the bows. Miss Fairey Bell had many tiny bows, like the ones on the front of brassieres, tied to tiny tufts of her hair.

Miss Fairey Bell also had a passion for hard candy, especially sour balls. She had a creative way of augmenting the meager supply her plump embarrassed daughter brought her every month.

She kept a bowl of marbles in her top drawer.

When Miss Fairey Bell was at the end of her sour balls, I'd make it a point to visit her, to see her take the marbles out of the drawer and say to me, "Sour ball, honey?"

The first time I was stunned. As politely as I could, I said, "No, thank you ma'm".

"Well, I think I will," she said, popping a marble into her mouth and swallowing it. Another followed. I could hardly believe my eyes. How lucky could a little girl be to live in a house where people ate marbles?

When the maids found out about Miss Fairey Bell's sour ball substitute they made crude jokes and comments that even Grandmother smiled at a little. She actually guffawed when one of them said it was easy to tell when Miss Fairey Bell was sitting on the toilet because you could hear her "Ping, Ping."

Although I had never actually heard it, I could lure other kids home with promised sightings of marble swallowing. Seeing us slip into her room, Miss Fairey Bell, as generous and gregarious as ever, was sure to say, "Honey, would you care for a sour ball?"

I had instructed any urchin there to refuse politely. Most just shook their heads, satisfied just to be a part of such arcana. "Well, I believe I will have one," and Miss Fairey Bell would open the drawer and take out the bowl of marbles, swallowing one or two right on cue.

My little compatriot would invariably look at me in wide-eyed admiration before we excused ourselves and left. Few ever returned for a second visit. Once their mothers found out they had been in the presence of marble-swallowing crazy folks, that was the end of visits. I felt very sorry for these kids in their small, boring homes with their boring families.

Billy Coburn had my Blue Diamond out of the Tube Rose can, hacking off great curls of bark from the crepe myrtle, uncaring of either the design or the damage. True, I had done my share of carving on the tree with the razor blade, but mine was not random slashing. The smooth, taffy-colored bark of a crepe myrtle, about an eighth of an inch thick, makes the trunk of the tree look as if it were made of flesh instead of wood. A child could carve an everlasting scar into it with a sharp piece of glass, much less a real blade. With my Blue Diamond I had carefully cut my initials, various dates that seemed important at the time, a couple of hearts joined with an arrow, and a modification of my current naughty word ("do-do"), not daring to render into bark the real word.

Carving the crepe myrtle was a joy. The front part of the razor blade went easily through the bark to the cambium. With bark so smooth, it was simple to score another line beside the first one and lift out the sliver of bark to expose a line of cambium. The most fumble-fingered child could carve three initials in minutes, and do it well enough to pass for the work of a teenager.

Tired of carving, I could either sit in the tree and read my Batman comics, with a flannel baby blanket tied around my neck billowing out behind me like Batman's cape, or grab the rope I had tied to a higher limb and swing out into space, just like Batman.

Now here was Billy in my sacred tree, in my hiding place, slashing at the bark with abandon. Picking up the biggest dirt clod I could find I flung it at him, striking only a glancing blow off his cheek and the bridge of his nose. But grains of sand and red dirt got into his eye.

Billy bellowed. He almost lost his footing, but not his grip on the Blue Diamond. I could see it in his fingers. He reached for my rope to swing down to the ground, and I knew there would be a confrontation I could never win. I didn't care. Wild with anger, I didn't budge.

Billy stuck the Blue Diamond into the tree to take the rope in both hands. What happened next was so unexpected it seemed blurred. I don't know if Billy's hand slipped on the rope or his foot slipped on the tree, but he seemed to hang a moment in the air, then he plummeted down like a stone. My eyes followed his progress toward the earth, then jerked back upwards to find him hanging by his head from the crotch of two crepe myrtle limbs, kicking like crazy and trying to reach the main trunk with his feet for support. His hands were on the limbs beside his head, but his strength was not enough to pull his body up. His noggin was stuck as tight as you please.

It would be nice to report that I went over and braved Billy's flailing feet and his wrath to help him down from the tree, but that would be a lie. I would like to report that I set my childish rage aside and at great cost to myself tried to unjam Billy's head and save his life. Nothing would be further from the truth.

Noticing Billy's kicking getting slower and his skin taking on a definite bluish cast, I turned and took my sweet time walking across the lawn, into the house to Grandmother's kitchen. She was washing kale in the sink. I watched her search for the green cabbage loopers that afflicted kale, and saw her intensity break as she looked out the window.

"Becca, what's that hanging in the crepe myrtle tree?" she honked. She paused to clean her glasses on her apron and added, "If you leave another baby blanket out in the rain, I'm not going to give you another." Putting her glasses back on she refocused. "That looks like Billy Coburn, Becca."

I pulled my chair up to the sink to look out the window. "Yes'm."

"Is he hanging in the tree, Becca?"

"Yes'm." I was a truthful child.

"My God..." She wheeled and charged outside as quickly as her old legs with ridges and humps and blue veins would carry her.

Putting my chair back under the table just so, I sashayed across the yard, not in a hurry. She was struggling, not with Billy's weight, which was not great; even I could have lifted him. The problem was that his head was wedged in the limbs so tightly she couldn't get him loose. But he breathed again when she supported his body and started to snuffle and wail. "Becca, get LL. And Becca, run this time," she puffed. She was on to me. She knew. I don't know why I was surprised. I could only hope it wouldn't get more complicated by her finding the razor blade.

I almost ran out of my shoes toward the back of the house. Grandfather and a guard clumped back behind me, without much enthusiasm at first. They thought I was exaggerating. At the sight of Billy hanging by his head and poor tired Grandmother supporting him, they ran too.

Grandmother knelt beside Billy on the lawn, moving his head back and forth, examining the chafed places under his ears, on the backside of his jaws and on the nape of his neck. Billy was getting pinker and his breathing more regular.

After a bit he sat up by himself and looked around in the same dumb way a bird does after flying into a window pane. He got slowly to his feet and steadied himself. With speed no one thought him capable of, he lashed out a kick at Grandmother that caught her on the ankle. Turning, he spat a big hocker at Grandfather.

Grandfather's face blazed. He made a small movement toward the boy, now beginning a wobbly run toward the edge of the yard. Grandfather caught himself and started laughing. "Yessireebob, I guess that's the last time that little boy'll come on the property."

Grandmother fastened her eyes on me. I moved back on the lawn, away from the tree and the illegal blade. "Becca, didn't you know Billy was hanging from the crepe myrtle?"

"Yes, ma'm."

"Why didn't you say something to me sooner?" I looked to Grandfather for support.

"For Chri'sake, Cornelia, she probably thought she was doing the world a favor if the little bastard choked." He turned to me. "Gal, you let us know as quick as you can when something like this happens again." I nodded, wide-eyed. He swatted me lightly on the rear and I walked hand in hand between them back to the house.

The razor blade, that Blue Diamond that was to be such a friend in the future, was still sticking in the tree. Adults didn't see everything.

School was a splendid example of that. Atrocities took place on the playground with deadening regularity. Girls whipped at each other with jumpropes, boys pummeled the shoulders and arms of other boys while the teachers stood together in a little group talking. Occasionally, for a major disaster like Boyd Ballentine's accident on the slide, they'd be forced from ennui into action.

Boyd was a third grader, already fat as a butterball. Almost five feet tall at eight years of age, he outweighed a couple of the teachers. A nice enough kid, he was usually called Big Boyd, although a few kids called him "Fatty."

On the warm autumn day in question, Big Boyd had undulated across the school yard in his baggy short pants and climbed the ladder to the top of the slide, gleaming from the polishing of thousands of child bottoms and waxed paper saved from luncheon sandwiches. Children, big kids mostly, would sit on the waxed paper at the top of the slide to get a faster ride.

Big Boyd took not one, but two pieces of waxed paper from the massive lunch his mother had sent with him, placing one sheet under each cheek. A hush fell over the assembled urchins as he started his ride. Boyd flew down the slide. A split second into his descent a splinter on the side rail caught Boyd's tubby leg just at the knee. It lay the flesh of his leg open to his waist, ripping his shorts to the waistband as his weight and momentum drove him toward the earth. He landed in the middle of a knot of stunned children. "Mama," he bawled. In the silence the word sounded like a train wreck.

The teachers bolted over, pushing silent children aside only to recoil at what they saw. Strangely, there was hardly any bleeding for the size of the cut. The edges of the wound gaped open. Instead of smooth muscle, what we saw was yellowish fat, just like at hog-killing time. One of the teachers leaned on the fence and lost her lunch. Miz Andrews, Boyd's teacher, ran into the office to call Dr. Grey. Miss Spruill sent one of her biggest second graders over to the service station to get her father who worked there.

It took the other teachers only about two minutes to get all the open-mouthed children off the playground and back into the classrooms. As we lined up to go inside, the men from the service station were running into the playground, as were Boyd's mother and Dr. Grey. Some of the big third grade boys pressed into service when Boyd had to be taken down to Dr. Grey's office told us later what happened.

Boyd couldn't walk, and he couldn't be taken in a car. The service station men picked up Boyd and placed him on a door they had taken off a coat closet. Since they were old and Boyd and the door were heavy, they recruited some of the bigger boys to help carry Boyd to the doctor's office. Miz Hardison, our teacher, let us stand at the window and watch as Boyd and his entourage left the playground.

Miz Andrews' class was also in our room, looking out the window, transformed by the dignity and solemnity of the occasion. They knew, as children do, that they had achieved a bit of immortality by just being in Big Boyd's room. One of their very own had been cruelly struck down. They would report it to mothers and siblings. Neighbors would question them. They would be worthy messengers.

The procession moved smartly off the playground and down the sidewalk. About a dozen of the biggest third grade boys carried the closet door on their shoulders. Miss Spruill's father from the service station held up the front of the door and his mechanic the back part. Boyd's jacket was balled up under his head and a white sheet covered his body.

Miz Andrews and Dr. Grey led the way down the sidewalk toward the doctor's office, walking briskly, kicking their way through the yellow and orange maple leaves, pretending to pay no attention to the cars that stopped on the street and the people who ogled from yards along the way. They were on a mission.

Boyd looked positively regal, lying on the closet door, borne along in the brilliant autumn sun looking for all the world like a fallen general. A corpulent one to be sure, but king-like under his sheet. As bearers of this stricken warrior, the third grade boys were glorified, in a scene straight from a Phantom comic strip. It wasn't often that such drama visited our drab town. In fact no one could remember having been actual witness to such tragedy and suffering.

The returning bearers were the center of attention of children and teachers at last recess. They told us that Dr. Grey said it looked worse than it was. They had watched Boyd get a couple of shots, one for lock jaw, the other to kill the pain. More than anything else, it was the news of two shots that got our attention. Children hate shots.

The boys saved the best for last. Using a huge needle, Dr. Grey had taken stitches — 42 in all, of thick black thread — right through Boyd's meat to close the wound. We were speechless, glad to see workmen from the superintendent's office already working on the slide to put an end to the episode.

At the first of the school year I had decided that Miz Hardison, our teacher, probably couldn't read, and that was why she was the first grade teacher. She had divided us into three groups for reading circles: the Rockets, the Bombers, and the Piper Cubs. She would take out thin little paperback books and labor over each and every phrase and word.

Reading circle became mind-numbing. Since I was in the Piper Cub group that read after lunch most days I could hardly stay awake. Neither could the rest of the Pipers. Even Miz Hardison seemed to want to nod off occasionally.

Mean Jimmy Speight had taught me to read years ago. I had my own library card since I was four years old when Grandmother realized I could read. Now and then in reading class, feeling a surge of compassion for the poor non-readers and Miz Hardison, I'd make up interesting stories about the pictures on whatever page we were belaboring. I didn't do it often, however, because Miz Hardison would cut her eyes all around and the other children would look at me like I was crazy.

Mean Jimmy never cut his eyes. From the first, when I started badgering him about reading the funny page in the newspaper, he started pointing out words. Prince Valiant and The Phantom were my passion.

Jimmy pointed at words, and when I could recognize one, he'd cut it out and put it in a Tube Rose can. Every day before we read the funny page, Jimmy made me get my can so we could review the little cut-out words inside. The Tube Rose cans were never completely free of snuff, and many a time when I shook my little cache of words onto the porch step where we worked, I would sneeze, creating a blizzard of funny-paper words.

Jimmy insisted that I line them up in a particular order, all the "A's" together, then the "B's", and so on, then read each of the little columns of words. If I missed any, even on the first try, Jimmy would put the word into his pocket, never to be seen again. I would have to earn it at another sitting. He was a very exacting and firm teacher.

We would read Prince Valiant and The Phantom together, he first, pointing out new words with his good hand. Then I would read. It wasn't long before I found I had a knack for reading, and that I could take the words from my can and make my own stories.

Grandmother beamed at Mean Jimmy when she discovered what we had been doing. The next day she bought him a large can of Tube Rose and a Zippo lighter with the Coast Guard insignia on it. It was Jimmy's turn to beam. He had a brother in the Coast Guard. "You have to teach her to write, too, Mr. Speight," Grandmother told him. She always called the inmates, white and black alike, by their formal names. To back up her request, she bought him a box of white stick chalk.

Jimmy would stand on the ground with his body propped against the edge of the porch to write. But the words he wrote, rounded off and hooked together, didn't look one whit like those in the funny paper. Discouraged, I burst into tears, not knowing the words to tell him what was wrong. "Write it in Prince Valiant writing, Jimmy," I blubbered, frustrated.

He and Grandmother understood at the same moment. "She needs to have it printed, Mr. Speight."

Then the words I knew started flowing out of the end of Mean Jimmy's chalk. I almost wept with relief, seeing my word friends there in chalk on the porch.

If Jimmy was a firm teacher when it came to reading, he was a task master at writing. Every day before we actually wrote words we practiced marks, starting with straight marks first: "llllll". Then we made circles: "OOOOOOOO". After we had filled the length of the porch between the two left pillars with those marks we wrote actual letters.

I was an eager student, hesitating only when he said we would write "bowels." He seemed quite serious. I had had a recent and devastating experience with bowels and was not about to start until I knew what he meant.

Grandmother kept a large box of Ex-Lax 'way up in a kitchen

cabinet. She had told me a hundred times not to touch it, that it wasn't candy. Chocolate was my passion, though, and the day she took the box down to get Ex-Lax for one of the inmates and left it on the counter was a day to remember. I could reach it just by standing on a chair. First I took out the tinfoiled squares and looked at them. Then I made tiny cuts with my thumbnail through the silver wrappers, leaving a train of little brown crescents. I loved the way the thin tinfoil retained the impression of the writing on the candy, but I couldn't read then.

With all the handling and just a little coaching from a chubby finger, an edge of the foil came up from a corner and I licked it. No doubt about it, it was candy. Why was Grandmother lying? After eating half the box I decided that Ex-Lax would never be a real challenge to Hershey's, but it was close enough when the real item wasn't available. It didn't take me long to eat the rest. I stuffed the tinfoil into the box and started across the kitchen to find a hiding place for it when, for the first time I could remember, I pooped my pants. I took a step toward the door and pooped again. Then I was pooping with every step I took, and bellowing at the top of my lungs.

Aunt Martha got to me first and sized up the situation, assuming I had an intestinal upset. She was putting institutional-strength pine-scented disinfectant into the water in a mop bucket when Grandmother came in. Stripping me down on the spot, she put my little blue dress into a bucket of sudsy water when the empty Ex-Lax box floated to the top of the water, clearly visible through the suds. Grandmother fished it out and held it up for Aunt Martha to see. "O Lordy," Aunt Martha moaned.

"Where is the Ex-Lax, Becca?" Grandmother asked. I looked at the counter, hoping there'd be a piece I'd missed still there, starting to snuffle again. The exertion inspired another round of diarrhea.

Aunt Martha hopped up and scanned the counter, but found nothing. Grandmother wrapped me in a clean towel and yelled for Annie. "Annie, Becca has eaten a whole box of Ex-Lax. I need Martha to watch her in the tub while I get Dr. Grey on the phone."

Annie nodded and took the mop from Aunt Martha. "If you need some paregoric, I have plenty, Miz LL."

"It might come to that, Annie."

Aunt Martha sat me on the toilet while she drew water in the big footed tub. She put me in the right place. I pooped so often I was beginning to feel weak. Grandmother came into the bathroom and told Aunt Martha to get Annie's paregoric. Dr. Grey had gone to Pea Ridge to deliver a baby and the phone lines didn't go that far yet. Paregoric was called liquid cork. It would stop the diarrhea for sure, and she knew she'd have to get liquids into me to guard against dehydration.

Paregoric was a Southern mother's best friend. Put it on your finger and smooth it onto a teething baby's gums and it would ease the pain. It stemmed diarrhea and menstrual pain. Best of all it turned children, from babies to teenagers, into well-mannered people who could sit still and listen and say "Yes, Ma'm". A large enough dose would help a child slip into an afternoon nap long enough to allow a mother to play a couple of rubbers of bridge.

Paregoric was an over-the-counter medication, though laced with morphine. Even some who worried about the effects of the morphine used it anyway for respite from crabby children. Having well-behaved, passive children often outweighed any danger the drug might pose, as children sat like dreamy little angels for hours at the time.

I passed a somnolent 48 hours. Grandmother and Aunt Martha woke me up periodically to make sure I drank some of Grandmother's punch. My tongue was purple for a week from the amount I drank but gradually I regained control of my bowels and lost my craving for chocolate and punch.

Mean Jimmy wrote the vowels on the porch in chalk, chanting, "Big A, little a. Big E, little e." He would make the lines just so, incorporating the circles and lines we had practiced. Soon into writing lessons, it occurred to me that the letters we were drawing on the porch were the same ones Grandmother and I used when we talked with our fingers. I never really discussed it with Jimmy, because he didn't talk that way.

When Miz Hardison started with those little paper books in first grade, I assumed she could read neither letters nor fingers. That's why I tried to pep things up with my stories. Meanwhile the Bombers and the Rockets whizzed right along into books a bit more interesting. I knew, because I listened as their groups read.

Just before Halloween something happened that changed my fortune for a good two years. We got our first *Weekly Reader.* The words in the little newspaper were not new to me, but I was enthralled by the concept: A newspaper for babies! I read the whole thing, even the publication information and the editor's note to the teacher.

Miz Hardison collected the little newspapers for more work the next day. Thinking we were finished with them, I worried that she had forgotten the material in the editor's note. After all the children had gone for the day I went back inside, so anxious I could hardly speak. When she finally acknowledged me I reminded her ever so quietly about the information in the editor's note. "How did you know about that, Becca?" She didn't seem angry.

"It said it right there in the Editor's Note to Teachers, Miz Hardison."

She handed me one from her desk. "Show me what you mean, Becca." I opened the paper to the third page and read the note. I could see she liked the reading, so I read the publication date and where *Our Weekly Reader* was published. Her face was pink. She sat me back down in my chair and told me to wait for her. When she returned, she and the third grade teacher were carrying a stack of books. I read the word lists in the back of each book quite easily. I knew the teachers were pleased, even though they did not say so.

The Piper Cubs had to limp along without me after that day. In fact, I never was placed in another reading group, but allowed to read anything I wanted at any time of the day. When visitors came to the classroom, my teacher would introduce me as if I were a little wunderkind, a virtuosa of the printed word. If they asked me to, I would read aloud. My ability made my first few years of school truly golden.

Later, when my father came home, reading helped me spin a cocoon around my body and mind. Reading allowed me the only safety and respite that I knew during those years.

The sailors and soldiers came home to parades. Children held balloons while bands played and everyone cheered. We saw this when Aunt Elsie drove us to Norfolk to get my father and mother. Mother had timed it so that her train from San Francisco arrived about the same time as my father's ship, which had to come through the Panama Canal. Everyone seemed to be in a festive mood, but I felt like a stranger at someone else's party.

When the cheering stopped, the women who had taken jobs at the mill for the most part returned home. A few kept working, the ones with office jobs.

My father took his old job back at the mill. He and my mother moved into Grandmother's apartment at the Home while they looked for housing. Plimpton, with its paper mill, was just a few miles from the Home. With all the returning service men and the mill gearing up to its capacity, housing was very scarce.

My first indication of the extent of his hatred toward me occurred soon after he came home. We were all sitting at the big dining room table groaning from the effects of Grandmother's noon meal. I got up to fetch something, skipping past him to get it.

"Sit down!" He absolutely roared at me. No one had ever spoken to me that way. I stood there, stunned.

Before I could move, he leaned back in his chair and hit me with the back of his hand. I didn't know to duck or move; I had never been hit before. His hand caught me on my left cheek, the force of the blow lifting me from my feet. I crashed into the wall behind me. The blow may have knocked me unconscious, or perhaps it knocked the wind out of me, but when I became conscious of my surroundings, I realized my mouth was bleeding and I had wet my pants. I sat there gasping, mortified. Nothing like this had ever happened to me.

I didn't know what to do.

Grandmother leapt to her feet to help me. "Leave her alone!" he roared. "She's got to learn some manners. You've let her run wild here."

Grandmother pushed past him and picked me up. I stayed away from him as best I could from then on.

About a week later, while taking a taking a bath in Grandmother's big tub, the door suddenly opened behind me. In the mirror of the medicine chest I saw him standing there. I froze. Had I been singing? Had he heard the water splashing? I wracked my brain to think how I might have offended him. I cowered behind the bathcloth, not knowing what to do.

"I'm going to see if you bathe yourself correctly," he said. He glanced at the door, then locked it.

"Well, stand up," he said. I stayed frozen. He reached into the tub and dragged me to my feet. Getting the bathcloth, he began to scrub my body. Nobody had bathed me since I was five. I felt a monstrous danger near. I stood motionless, my head down, hoping I would live.

He examined my body, soaping his hands and running them over me. He was breathing through his mouth. He got up to leave. "If you tell your mother, I'll kill you," he said.

I sat down in the tub, too afraid to cry.

5

Did I actually hear it or did I imagine it? Was Aunt Martha really in the hall? To this day I do not know, but I certainly thought she was there. Wherever she was that first night my father sexually molested me, she was not in the house the next morning.

Angry and hostile words swirled around the breakfast table. I tried to be the perfect child, keeping my eyes on my plate, chewing with my mouth closed. I kept my elbows off the table and my napkin in my lap. In silence I ate every bite on my plate. When I finished, I placed my knife and fork across the top edge of my plate, just as the adults did. The knife fell off. Without breaking his train of thought or hesitating in his speech, my father slapped me out of my chair. "Charles, you will never do that again at my table," Grandmother said. She looked around. "Martha?"

"That black bitch is gone. She'll never touch this child again."

Grandmother came around the table and helped me to my feet. "You will be gone, too," she told him. "Whether you have found your new house or not, you will be out of here in two weeks."

I clung to her, relieved that he was going to go. It didn't occur to me at first that I would have to go with him.

He reached over and grabbed my arm. "Go to your room." As I walked toward the door, I passed my mother, still picking at her food. She hadn't raised her eyes or acknowledged my presence.

It never occurred to me to appeal to her. She was still an outsider to me. I didn't think of her as my mother. She wasn't like other mothers I had seen, like Mrs. D'Autremont, caring for their children even when they were disciplining them.

My mother was the most passive person I have ever known. From the time she married my father right out of high school, she allowed herself to be totally dominated by him. He gave her instructions as to where she should live while he was off to sea, and she obeyed. He told her to leave their child behind, and she did so. Did she ever have any thoughts of her own? If so, she never said anything to make me believe it.

Now I sat on the edge of my bed trying not to wrinkle the counterpane. As I listened for his footsteps, I wondered where I would hide if I heard him coming.

The knowledge that Aunt Martha was gone was numbing. I felt absolutely bereft without her protection. I had never even dreamed that she would not be there for me, as much a part of the house as the walls or the stove. Someone else would start the fire. Would she let me sit in the chair with arms carved like the heads of swans? Would she let me watch as she made the biscuits?

I could hear the bread tray against the counter as Aunt Martha worked it. The flour she sifted into the tray drifted like snowy ridges. She pulled the lard stand from the pantry, scooping curls of white shortening from it, never measuring, always knowing just how much. She cut it through the drifts of flour, creating a crater in the middle for the milk from the big jug in the cooler.

She never measured the milk, either, always just enough for the flour and lard, just enough to moisten all the other ingredients, to make them a cohesive mass. Aunt Martha kneaded the mass, as big as a baby and at least as heavy, with an economy of motion that came with years of repetition. She folded the dough, pushing against it with the heels of her hands. Detecting the slightest variance of moisture she would take a handful of flour, scattering it as if sowing wheat, always feeling for the proper balance.

She kneaded the dough deftly until it felt as smooth and cool as the flesh of my grandmother's upper arm, the part nearest her body.

Some women, white ones mainly, would roll their dough out with a rolling pin and cut it in perfect circles, with a uniformity they seemed to require in their lives. Aunt Martha would never cut dough. She'd pull out a little lump that seemed about right, then squeeze the lump off onto the bread tray. With quick hands and sure fingers she'd reduce the big lump of dough into its fifty or sixty component lumps in almost no time, then roll each one in her palms, her right palm cupped over her flattened left one, finally dropping the dough on the black baking pan used only for this purpose. To the untrained eye they looked alike, but to us they were as individual as fingerprints, just the right shade of brown on top and barely crusty on the bottom, fluffy inside and white as mashed potatoes. A plume of vapor escaped into the air when one was pulled apart, ready for a pat of butter, a sugary preserved fig, or a wash of gravy. Who would make the biscuits now?

As I listened, I heard my mother's high heels in the hall before being muffled by the living room rug. She was going out. With Aunt Martha gone, I expected the worst. How much I had taken her protection for granted!

Now I heard his footsteps, coming toward my room. I listened for the sound of Grandmother's shoes, lace-up Dr. Scholls with chunky heels, but didn't hear them. He was on the way to my room. Would he beat me for dropping my knife? I sat on the counterpane I had just smoothed with my little eight year old hands, trying not to let the tears behind my eyes come onto my face. He hated tears.

He opened my door and stood watching me. I cowered, expecting the slap, the hard hand across my face, as he walked toward me. Instead, he grabbed me by the upper arms and stood me on the bed. Slowly, breathing heavily, he began to take off my clothing. He pulled at my little girl nipples. He spread my legs, examining my mons, pulling at my labia.

I yearned for the war to start again, another war with the Nazis. Could Nazis be this bad? Could they have hurt little girls like this man, my father?

I also cursed myself, for not realizing the protective power of Aunt Martha's magic. Where was the feather necklace she had made me? The bones strung together for protection? The bits of mirror reflecting evil, the salt sifted along the window sill to keep out the haints?

When the big hurricane came during the war, we hadn't been warned because of the news blackout. Even though it was October, just past the height of the hurricane season, not even the old heads picked up a hint of hurricane, much less this monster, from radio weather reports. It blew straight from Africa and into the Gulf of Mexico. The summer had been a scorcher and the big hurricane lapped up the heat stored in the blue gulf water like cane sugar. It sat in the gulf, churning. By October when the sky turned the color of an old bruise, almost all the crops were barned. The tobacco, old sotweed money plant, had been sold in August and September; Tarboro and Wilson smelled like humidors. Some farmers had stock peas left in the fields, but it was mainly browse for the deer and food for quail in their Autumn coveying.

Barometer watchers noticed the column of mercury dip and began to batten down, more from force of habit than actual danger. "Too late for anything big," they muttered to themselves, but habit was strong and they did the work.

Two days of heavy rain filled the Chowan and the Roanoke, making them flow faster, moving rainwater into the Sound. The entire Coastal Plain sucked up the water like a sponge, widening creeks, moving water.

The County Home stood on the highest spot in the county, thirteen feet above sea level, bounded on the East by 'Scape Ho Swamp between the prison fields and Kendricks Creek two miles away. 'Scape Ho had been named before the Revolutionary War, when the area provided the naval stores for shipping tar, turpentine, pitch, and big timbers for keels and spars back to England. Boats came up the Roanoke from the Atlantic, their hulls mossy and sails mildewed. The fresh water of the river killed the dense growth on the hulls while the sails bleached on the river banks. Sailors had time on their hands and money in their pockets. According to legend, one woman took the money but had provided no service. After her arrest she managed to escape into the swamp, giving it its name: 'Scape Ho.

Some say swamps make the hair raise on their arms, but I never felt that way. I loved 'Scape Ho, the big, buttressed cypresses sending up Disneyesque knees through mushy black earth and the clear, still water the color of pekoe tea. I loved the life it supported, like the many different kinds of fish, some journeying in from the sea in silver drifts just to spawn in the fresh water. Mud turtles lined up on half-submerged logs, plopping into the water like so many Busby Berkeley dancers, one by one, at the approach of danger. There were fifty different kinds of frogs, blizzards of butterflies and birds, and a profusion of plant life from veils of Spanish Moss to tiny orchids with blossoms the size of a thumbnail and little strap-like leaves living on horizontal branches with Resurrection ferns.

And there were snakes, little green ones that came up into the yard and black ones that lived in the barns, dear to the hearts of farmers for devouring rats. Vipers abounded, too. Rattlesnakes were kind, buzzing a warning to a child too close. Moccasins and copperheads depended on the good sense and sharp eyes of the encroacher but would try to move away if given time. Even though 'Scape Ho Swamp was full of snakes, I never knew anyone who was actually bitten by one.

Grandmother, keen to the weather as any coastal native, bought kerosene for the lamps and ordered extra ice. She had the trustees move almost a cord of wood into the living room beside the fireplace. The grumbling maids filled very jar and crock with water. "We can always pour it out," she honked.

After an afternoon sopping with humidity, the sunset was yellow before the wind picked up. By dark the rain had started again, but the power didn't go off until after dawn the next morning. The wind was now blowing about fifty knots. Trees were losing limbs. The barometer continued to fall. By the next afternoon the streets were flooded, but most of us had seen that before. The river would take care of the water. We were sure we were getting into the worst of it, and it would be over soon.

Grandmother could have made sandwiches for dinner, but the old people were becoming anxious and cold listening to the wind. Instead she served them a soothing dinner — pot roast with potatoes and carrots, bread and butter pickles, steaming bowls of collard greens with chunks of fatback and plates of fried cornbread. Since the big stove didn't need electricity, it was business as usual for the kitchen crew.

Though October days were getting shorter, it was already dark at five o'clock the day the big hurricane hit. The long skinny windows with beveled panes that reached from floor to ceiling beside the double doors in the lobby were boarded up, but we watched the rain through the courtyard windows that were protected from the wind. By midnight the storm showed no sign of abating.

Captain Sexton, his eyes the funny blue color of skimmed milk, cocked his head listening. "She's blowing eighty knots out there," he told us. Captain Sexton had been retired from the merchant marines by his glaucoma, but we respected his authority when it came to weather.

In the morning I woke to the smell of bacon and coffee, and the sounds of wind shrieking and rainwater rumbling through downspouts. All the inmates were served in the white dining room that morning, the able-bodied helping the nonambulatory to the table. Even the small change of venue seemed to lift everyone's spirits. The candles on the table and the thin light from the courtyard window seemed to cheer everyone except Captain Sexton.

"Coffee'll get everything moving, Cap'n Sexton," Grandmother honked.

"Everything but that damned hurricane, Miz Bass. Git me the barometer if you will."

Grandmother helped him hold it close to his face.

"Goddamn these eyes," Captain Sexton raged, putting his fingers around his eye sockets as if to pluck them out.

Grandmother put her hands over his ever so gently. "I know

what you're going through, Cap'n Sexton." She hugged his head aginst her apron and rocked him the way she comforted me when my feelings were hurt.

"Cap'n Sexton," she honked, "tell you what. I'll be your eyes and you be my ears." The old sailor nodded and brightened a little. We all pretended not to see the tears on his cheeks.

"Read me the numbers, Cornelia." Sharing senses allowed familiarity.

"It's right around 29, Captain."

"I need precision, woman!" He smacked the arm of the wheel-chair with the flat of his hand.

"29 point 16," Grandmother replied smartly.

Captain Sexton stared into the distance past the glaucoma in his eyes, looking like the Oracle of Delphi. Snapping back into the present, he looked to where he thought Grandmother was. "The needle must have moved. It don't seem low enough. Did you check it on the wall, Cornelia?"

"It has a locking device, Mr. Sexton. I locked it into place before I moved it from the wall." I sidled up behind Grandmother to hear every word.

"Miz Bass, I need to speak with Cap'n LL.," he said in a conspiratorial voice. Grandmother hesitated. Grandfather was having coffee in their apartment, time he needed alone. Besides, he resented intrusion. She could sense Captain Sexton's urgency, though.

"I'll get a lamp," she said. I didn't need light to keep up with her down the long dark halls, staying close to the wall to avoid betrayal from creaking floor boards. Grandfather didn't hear me as I scooted past the kitchen where he sat drinking coffee. I knew Grandfather would never talk business in the kitchen, so I headed for the living room and dove into my hiding place behind the green wingback chair.

From my pitch-dark vantage point, I heard the rumbling of hard rubber wheels coming closer. Sure enough, the three adults entered the living room, Grandfather taking the oil lamp Mr. Sexton had balanced on his knees.

Mr. Sexton cleared his throat. "'Scuse this intrusion into your morning routine, Cap'n LL, but I have some urgent information for you 'bout this here storm."

"I 'preciate your taking your time to tell me about it, Cap'n Sexton. We all know when it comes to weather, you're the expert. Now, Cornelia's comin' with coffee and I'd appreciate it if you'd wait and tell her too."

Behind my wingback I knew the adults were afraid. They got very formal when danger was near. My skin prickled with fear. I wanted to leave my hideout and climb onto a lap for comfort, but if I revealed myself they would make me leave. I sat tight and listened.

When I heard Grandfather sugaring his coffee, I leaned against the back of the chair trying to feel his warmth. "What have we got on our hands here, Cap'n Sexton?"

"We got a big one out there, Cap'n LL. If I don't miss my guess it's as big as the cyclones in the East China Sea."

"What are the signs, Cap'n Sexton? The winds are hurricane force, but we've seen worse."

Captain Sexton wasn't angered by the affront to his authority. Indeed he seemed to wax on the interest. Leaning forward in his chair he said quietly, "Luther, it's been raining hard for three days. The swamps have been accommodatin' the flow and the rivers have been pushin' it on down to the Sound. The wind's been blowin' from the East Southeast.

The problem is the barometer hasn't fallen enough for as long as that storm's been here. As bad as it seems now, until the pressure goes way down from where it's at right now, we haven't yet seen the worst of it."

"What do you think is going to happen, Cap'n Sexton?"

"Could be it could turn across the Great Dismal Swamp and kick the shit out of Norfolk. We'd get a lick and a promise if it did that."

"Or?"

"It could come on in here."

"What would be your educated guess, Cap'n Sexton?" Grandmother honked.

"I think we're gonna git it, Cornelia."

The living room was quiet. Captain Sexton's words inspired credence. The adults would be sitting with that look in their eyes that said they had a million things to do and their responsibilities seemed too big.

A spoon jangled against a saucer. My grandparents jumped to their feet quickly. "His medicine's in his breast pocket," Grandmother said, letting the back of the chair down as Grandfather searched for the medicine. The bottle held about four ounces of fluid, elixir of digitalis. Grandfather pulled the stopper and squeezed the bulb to draw liquid into the glass dropper.

"How much, Cornelia?"

"Six drops. On the back of his tongue."

"Goddammit, I can't see."

"I'll hold the lamp, Grandfather." I was out of the hideout, wanting to see how Captain Sexton was. My grandparents exchanged a long look before Grandfather nodded. Very still, I held the lamp near Captain Sexton's mouth. Grandfather counted the drops as they slid down the old man's throat. Grandmother worked on the leg holders of the chair, getting the captain's legs straight out.

Slowly color returned to Captain Sexton's face. His fingernails started to lose the bluish tinge of his eyes in favor of their accustomed pink. "Listen, old man, you can't weigh anchor on us now. You've got to stay with us while we ride this thing out. A lot of lives depend on the three of us, Captain."

I was open-mouthed at Grandfather's eloquence and gentleness, and noticed a funny light in Grandmother's eyes. The blood had long since run from my arms from holding the lamp high; when I wavered, Grandfather took the lamp from me and gave me a scratchy morning-beard kiss. "You did mighty fine holding that lamp, Becca. You might have to do that again." My little being expanded with importance. For once I was speechless.

Captain Sexton motioned to be set up straight again. Grandfather lowered his legs while Grandmother raised his head. They waited for him to adjust to being upright. Captain Sexton's weak voice whispered, "LL, this is what I think'll happen. That thing is a monster. It's layin' out there just inside the Outer Banks, churning away. The tide is high now and the water's backin' up in the rivers and the Sound. High as the water is out there now, it's gonna get higher. I reckon if it's gonna come on in, it'll be on the next high tide this evenin'."

Grandfather's face was grave. Grandmother bit her lip.

"You ain't seen high water, LL. You gotta git them families out of the guards' houses. 'Scape Ho can't begin to handle this kind of water. And LL, you gotta get them convicts up here or they're gonna drown like caged rats in them cells." Turning blue again, Captain Sexton leaned back from the exertion of speaking. Without asking, Grandfather got the elixir out of Captain Sexton's breast pocket and dripped more medicine into the old man's mouth.

"Careful with that, LL. Dr. Bray said too much could kill him."

"We'll take care of it, Cap'n Sexton. We'll start on it now."

"The water's gonna start comin' up 'bout four o'clock. The worst of it'll come in by evenin'. You got 'bout ten hours to get things straight, LL."

The four of us marched back down the hall, Grandfather pushing the Captain's wheelchair and Grandmother walking beside. I led, carrying the lamp. Grandfather stopped us for a moment before entering the lobby. "Cornelia, we'll put the guards' families in our apartment, one family in each room. The white prisoners can stay in the colored lobby, and the colored prisoners in the colored dining room. We'll use the main lobby and the white dining room for the old folks." Grandmother nodded.

He continued, "I'm going to pull out the ice and whatever food we can move from the prison up here, and turn the kitchen over to Beau Lef'. God knows, he ain't gonna bother the maids. Beau Lef' can take care of the trustees, see that they serve the prisoners. The maids will take care of the old folks. You're gonna have to take care of the guards' families as well as the old folks, Cornelia. Can you do that?"

"Of course I can." Her fingers talked along with her voice, betraying her outward calm. "I'll have Martha lay a fire in the colored lobby. The prisoners'll be wet to the skin walking up here. I'll..." She hesitated. Putting her arms around Grandfather she hugged him and clung to him. "I'll take care of things on this end," she promised.

"Cornelia, I'll have a guard with a shotgun with the families. Nothing will happen, I promise you. And we'll guard the prisoners while they're in the house."

She nodded in agreement. We went into the lobby. "Annie, get all the maids into my living room. You come too, Martha." Eyes widened, looks were passed. Annie went to get the other maids while Grandmother went back to her kitchen to make more coffee.

When it was ready she took the coffeepot into her living room where the nine maids were sitting stiffly. She served each of them, asking about cream and sugar, then served herself and sat down. Taking a sip of her coffee, she sent her gaze around the room. "I really need your help." She said it simply and, for her, quietly. The nine other women nodded. Her seriousness was unmistakable. They sat back in their seats.

"Captain Sexton says we haven't even seen a hurricane yet. He says what we are experiencing now is just the edge of what is coming. The water should rise more by evening. If that happens, the families in the guards' housing will be in real trouble, so I'm invitin' them up to stay in my apartment."

The maids almost gasped. Annie was the only one who had ever been in this part of the county home.

"We are going to keep the families in this part of the house. I need a volunteer to stay here with them." Grandmother nodded at a woman who raised her hand. "There will be a guard by the door leading to the big lobby at all times." Some women murmured, understanding what was to come. "The convicts have to come up from the prison. They'll occupy the colored inmate lobby and dining room."

The reality of what some had guessed brought another gasp. "Cap'n LL and the guards will be with them at all times. No maid will have to get near that area."

"What about the kitchen, Miz Bass? Who'll..."

"All food preparation will be done by the trustees."

Annie started chuckling. "Beau Lef'.....?"

"Beau Lef' will be our chef." Laughter swept through the room. Even Grandmother grinned. "We will count heads before and after

78

each meal..." The maids shrieked with laughter and dismay. This was a side of my grandmother I had never seen. She was making people laugh.

I knew about Beau Lef'. If he'd been white he would have been known as "light," a term used by genteel folks for a homosexual man. But Beau was very black, in prison for a grisly deed. He had been head chef at a renowned men's club in Philadelphia when Montgomery Collins, president of the Whispering Pines Club in Williamston, sampled Beau Lef's cuisine on a visit. He immediately determined to lure him South.

Montgomery Collins, Monty to his friends, was bisexual since his youth. He knew how to run a club. Monty promised Beau the moon and Beau moved South. Beau provided his white lover with food seldom seen in that part of the state. People came from as far north as Norfolk to eat at the Whispering Pines Club and from as far west as Raleigh. Anyone who had eaten anything besides barbeque ate there.

The night after Beau discovered that Monty's other lover was a white woman, Monty disappeared. The patrons at the Whispering Pines Club were dining on savory stews flavored with burgundy and herbs, choice roasts and chops, when a doctor dining there recognized one of the bones on his plate as being human and called the police. Positive identification was made by Monty's woman friend when they found his arms and hands in the ice house. She recognized the ring she had given him on his right hand. Since it was an onyx oval on a gold band, common for a man's ring, they had to check the inscription. The engraving consisted of a single word: "Big."

The diners from the club, the ones who could stop retching, wanted to lynch Beau Lef', but he was tried and sentenced to life. That's where Grandfather got him. He surely was an excellent cook, once you got past his brush with the law.

The guards' families moved into Grandmother's apartment first. Since there were eight families, Grandmother had to open a couple of extra rooms. They came with their cats and dogs; Grandmother couldn't bear the thought of those children losing everything. All told, after the last of the families moved in, there were 38 new people in that wing plus their pets.

Beau Lef' headed up the cadre of trustees coming in from the prison, followed by a guard with a shotgun. Grandmother served them coffee around the small table in the white dining room. They were as formal as the maids had been in Grandmother's living room, waiting to hear what was expected of them, why they were together in the white dining room.

Grandmother set her cup aside and started talking as if she were in a board meeting. "Gentlemen, the reason we are here...." She told them what Captain Sexton had said about the big storm and the high water coming. "We will not tolerate any loss of life to any of the convicts," she continued, "so we are moving all the prisoners up here to the main house." The men shifted in their chairs.

"If things are to proceed smoothly...," she bit her lip again and lowered her eyes, "we are going to need your help. I have one maid assigned to the guards' families in the North wing. Every single maid will be working 'round the clock seeing to the needs of the inmates who will be in the main lobby...."

Beau Lef' rose from his chair. He stood a full six foot three, his gigantic abdomen out in front of him like another entity. For all his size, his voice was modulated, almost sweet. "Miz Bass, I volunteer to take over the cookin'. You'll have your hands full overseein' everything." Holding his chin just so, he cut his eyes around the rest of the group. "I'm sure some of these boys will help out." As one, they all stood to volunteer. Grandmother beamed at them through her tears. "I assure you, ma'm, your kitchen will be left spotless and your maids unmolested." The trustees grinned.

Grandmother stood. "Well, thank you, Mr...ah, Lef'. Your help will be invaluable. Your reputation as a chef preceeds you."

"We 'preciate not being lef' to drown like rodents, Miz Bass." The rest of the trustees nodded.

"Let me show you the kitchen, Mr...ah, Lef'. I'm sure it's not what you're used to, but it is what we have to offer." The trustees stood together at the side of the room while Grandmother gave the cook the tour. It had been years since Beau Lef' had been in a well-stocked kitchen. He cooed when she showed him her spices, the exotic ones in big yellow cans with built-in lids that slid open and closed, and the ones she grew herself, hanging in dried bunches on racks in the pantry.

"Jesus, Mary, and Joseph, that can't be tarragon! You don't grow tarragon, Miz Bass!" Beau Lef' shrieked. He crossed himself before inhaling the gray-green hank hanging with the rest. He looked up from the bouquet of herbs in his big brown hands and said, "I smelled your lavender the moment I walked inside."

"I'll put some in a little sack for you when you leave, Mr., ah, Lef'."

"You call me 'Beau', Miz Bass. And put in a teensy, tiny pinch of that tarragon, too, if you can spare it."

Swooping past Grandmother into the kitchen, he ran his hand lovingly over the marble countertop. "Your pie and cobbler crusts are superb, aren't they, Miz Bass? I'll bet your cheese straws are divine."

"I don't make cheese straws. I roll out the cheese dough thin as a dime and cut wafers."

"Lots of cayenne?""

"You can see the flecks of red in the dough. And I added pecans chopped very finely."

Beau closed his eyes and smiled as if he had one in his mouth. He continued through the kitchen, making note of the large pots and pans. Almost casually he drew one of the big knives from the knife rack. It was Grandmother's favorite, of sharp gray metal with brass handle brads. Beau sighted down the blade, then tested it with his thumb and looked at Grandmother admiringly. "I should have known you'd keep your knives sharp, Miz Bass."

Grandmother's cheeks were pink. She had a look of triumph I had never seen before. "Well, shoot, Beau." Did she simper? "You call me 'Cornelia.'" For the first time, certainly not the last, I witnessed the phenomenon of the intense friendships between some southern women and some homosexual men.

"Cornelia," he said earnestly, "You go and take care of what you need to do. Me and the boys'll run this kitchen like a watch. We'll make it through this storm and eat like kings. People ain't so scared when their bellies are full. How many head'll be here for meals?"

"There's 38 people in the guards' families, Beau, and 8 guards. That's 46. Add Captain LL and Becca and me. 49. There are 58 old folks, white and black. That's 107 right there. How many convicts would you reckon are coming up?"

"All of 'em, Miz Bass. All 63," said one of the trustees.

"So that's an even 170." She stood, shaking her head slightly, realizing the enormity of the task. "Beau?"

"Yes, ma'm?"

"There's something else you should know."

"Yes, ma'm?"

"The guards' families brought their cats and dogs."

Grandmother and the trustees and Beau Lef' hooted and screamed with laughter, until tears ran down their faces and they doubled over with glee. There it was again: Grandmother was making people laugh!

"Six cats, five dogs." Her tally was greeted with more guffaws.

A trustee wiping his eyes said, "If the storm lasts too long, I guess we'll have a ready supply of food."

That didn't set well. Beau reached over and pinched the trustee's cheeks. "I've been thinking a lot about you, Pete....."

The trustee pulled away. "That ain't funny, Beau."

"Yes it is," answered Grandmother. "Carry on, Beau. I know you will. Be careful, Pete." She patted Beau on his arm and left them laughing.

By noon the maids had carried 63 twin sized mattresses to the colored lobby and the colored dining room. Each had a pillow, clean sheets and a flannel blanket.

The trustees had moved the hanging meat from the prison ice house up to the ice house behind the county home. Hams would spoil if water got to them. They hung them in the cold pantry. One went to the chicken house to collect eggs and chickens, taking the chicken cages to the wash house and the eggs to the kitchen.

"Luther, what about the stock?" Grandmother asked. "They're going to drown in that bottom land if the water gets as high as

Captain Sexton says."

"I'll take 'em to the North pasture, pigs and all. I'm gonna leave the gate open at the graveyard hill. If it gets that high, they can go in there. It's the best we can do."

"We could put 'em in the courtyard, Luther."

"I'm not bringing them beasts through the house, Cornelia. We got enough on our plates now without trying to walk pigs and cattle through the house to the courtyard. Both of us have enough to do now." Grandmother and I knew he was right, but her heart was so big and soft I knew she was hurting.

From the back porch I watched Grandfather and the trustees herd the pigs to the north pasture, then the cattle. The Jersey bull went last. I expected big trouble from him, but Grandfather clipped a lanyard into the ring in the big animal's nose and walked him, gentle as a lamb, to the North pasture. I noticed the wind blowing harder. The water was up from the swamp, into the flat fields behind the prison.

Grandfather took off his mac and left it in the lobby near the fire. He clumped down the white inmate hall to Captain Sexton's room. He was the only inmate left on the wing; every-one else was in the main lobby.

Grandfather stood at the door to Captain Sexton's room a moment. The old man's eyelids fluttered. "Crank this damn bed up, LL." Grandfather went to the foot of the bed to turn the crank. "Gimme a squirt of that elixir, so I kin talk to ye."

Grandfather took the bottle from the nightstand and placed the required drops into the old man's toothless mouth. Captain Sexton closed his milky blue eyes for a few minutes, waiting for the magic of the medicine. Grandfather and I looked at each other. Captain Sexton was dead, we thought. Finally the sheets moved. With his eyes still closed, he asked, "How bad is it, Cap'n LL?"

"The water's worse than anything. The tide's supposed to be mean low at 4:30. That's two hours from now, but the water hasn't shown a sign of receding. 'Scape Ho is full and up into the pasture behind the prison and the river is still up in the streets. The river ain't drainin' a bit and neither are the swamps and creeks. And now the

Sound seems to be blowin' up the river."

"The wind's still blowing from the East Southeast?"

Grandfather nodded and I nudged him. "Yes, sir," he said.

Captain Sexton listened quietly. "Sound's like she's blowing right at hurricane force."

"Has been for about 6 hours."

"I don't think she's going to turn, Luther. You watch that barometer and the minute she moves down a bit you'll know she's coming. As bad as that wind'll be, it'll be the water that'll git us."

"We got everything and everybody up here in the main house, Captain, the guards' families and even the convicts. Cornelia let the families bring their critters with 'em. She wanted to walk the stock through the house and corral them in the courtyard, but I drew the line at that. You know how she is, Captain."

The old man's face seemed to focus itself away from pain and into a grin. His rubbery old lips widened and parted to reveal gums exactly the color of bubble gum. He shook with laughter and folded his arms across his ribs to squeeze back the pain.

Grandfather grabbed the elixir from the nightstand and stood ready, but Captain Sexton didn't need it. "It must look like a goddamn ark in here, Luther."

"Space is gettin' scarce, Captain."

"Cornelia is gonna have her hands full cookin'. Did she put Martha and Annie in charge of the old folks?"

"Nope. She put one of the prisoners in charge in the kitchen."

Captain Sexton's old lips split into another grin before waving for Grandfather to come with the elixir. "God Almighty, Luther," he said after a pause. "Beau Lef' is gonna serve mankind again?"

"No, no. We're gonna keep a tally on who's here. We're gonna count before and after each meal. Becca's gonna be in charge of that."

"I'll relax, then. Beau prob'ly wouldn't want old stringy meat, anyway."

"He keeps eyeing Pete. Pete's been like a flea on a skillet since he got up here."

"What did you do with the stock, Luther?"

"I took 'em all to the north pasture, the hogs and cows, every-thing. That graveyard is on a little hill, so I left the gate open so they can get up high as they can. Maybe some of 'em 'll make it."

"I'm going to be joinin' 'em up there, Luther. It ain't gonna be much longer."

"Listen, Captain, you can't sail away on this watch. You stay here and help us through this thing."

The old man lay still. His lips said "Pppfff" a couple of times, so we knew he was asleep and not dead. We moved quietly to the door. "I'll stick as long as I can," the old man said, barely audibly.

Back in the main lobby, I watched Grandfather tap the domed glass over the dial of the barometer. "Has it moved?" I asked, not really knowing what would move.

"No," he said, turning to rehang it, then turning back to me. "This big hand is what we're watching, Becca. When the hurricane gets nearer, we'll know it's comin' because this hand will move lower on the dial." He pointed at a place below 28 where it would be. I nodded. I would watch.

Grandfather and I walked back down the hall to Captain Sexton's room. "It's mean low tide, Cap'n. 'Scape Ho is up to the vegetable garden behind the prison."

Captain Sexton seemed to sense my presence. "The...ah, crit-ters, they're comin' out of the swamp?"

"Yeah."

"You got the windows boarded up? That'll keep 'em out. And keep folks calm. What they eyes cain't see, they hearts won't grieve about." What was the old man talking about?

It was dark as night by 5 o'clock. Beau Lef' served the old folks first, sitting around the table in wonderment. "I just don't know what any of this stuff is," Mr. Suggs complained. He was always cross, more so when anything was different. Grandmother said it was because he had hemorrhoids. One of the trustees filled Mr. Suggs' plate with a generous scoop from the big pan with the flaky crust and set it before the grumpy old man. He opened his mouth to complain again, but a tiny fountain of saliva escaped instead, visible to most in the lamplight. Everyone laughed.

Mr. Suggs had seconds like everyone else. He smacked his lips when he tasted Beau's chocolate pie. "So, Mr. Suggs, it suits?" Beau already knew the answer.

"I guess it tastes all right," Mr. Suggs answered, a puff of meringue on the tip of his nose and a crumb of flaky crust on his chin, "but it don't *look* like Miz Bass's."

Beau tried a pirouette that made him look like a Walt Disney hippopotamus. "Neither do I!" he chirped.

As we moved the inmates back into the lobby I glanced at the barometer. It was dropping so fast I could almost see it move. I ran through the white dining room and into the kitchen, looking for Grandfather. When I started through the door to the colored dining room, Pete blocked my way. "You can't go in there, honey."

"I gotta, Pete," I pleaded with the trustee who so often had held my jumprope. "I have to tell him something."

Beau joined us, with steaming pans of food on a cart. "I'll take her in with me." I stood on the lower shelf and rode in with him, holding onto the handle. The prisoners looked up at our entry. Grandfather was just finishing his talk to them. "...and do not go out on the porch for any reason. The water is driving every livin' creature from the swamp. This house is on the highest spot in the county, but..."

He hesitated when he saw me with Beau. "I don't think I have to tell you that all these critters want to live. They're already in the cells. We don't want 'em inside here." He glanced again at me. Why did he seem annoyed? Was it that Beau had lifted me in his arms, up away from creatures that could come in while he was talking? "What is it, Becca?" His voice was sharp.

"Grandfather, the big hand on the weather clock is moving."

"Thank you, Becca," his voice kinder now. "Go and find Martha and stay with her." I ran to find her. Everyone seemed afraid. The wind sounded louder in the lobby than anywhere else in the house. Rain slashed at the porch roof and blew across to thrash the boarded-up windows.

Beau's good food and the excitement of the day were telling on the inmates and me. Aunt Martha scooped me up, cuddling me on her lap in a wooden rocker from the porch. "Listen to Aunt Martha, chile. She gotta tell you somethin'." My head was drooping from exhaustion, but I tried.

Taking a tattered cloth bag with a drawstring from her pocket she opened it. I could smell the garlic. "I don't want to wear a garlic necklace, Aunt Martha," I whined, crabby from having missed my afternoon nap.

"Not no garlic necklace, chile. This fo' yo' pockets." She slipped a head of garlic in each pocket of my pinafore. Next, she glanced around the room to see if anyone was listening. "Chile, the Death Angel be ovah dis house tonight. He be inside befo' mornin'." She pinned something to my shirt just below my chin. It was a small mirror glued to a piece of wood painted yellow. "De Death Angel see hisself in dis lookin' glass and fly away," she assured me.

She took a slender, pliable leather thong with a tiny bone tied to it and scattered a pinch of salt on it. "De vapors are runnin' from de storm," she said. Another thong held a feather. "From a sea harpy," she said. "No sea haint gonna come in heah with this aroun'."

Pulling a quilt over us both she began to rock. With each breath she whispered, "No Death Angel gonna git this chile. No Death Angel gonna git this chile."

I slept in the hell of noise from the storm and woke to the silence of its eye. Grandmother was standing over us with a lamp. "Martha," she mouthed, thinking it was a whisper. Aunt Martha and I followed her to the dining room. "Annie's been awake all night. I'll take Becca if you could spell her a while." Aunt Martha nodded, but I could tell she was worried. "Nothing'll happen to her, Martha." Grandmother pointed at my pin. "You gave her garlic, didn't you?"

Sheepish, Aunt Martha nodded. Grandmother patted her arm. We started down the hall to Captain Sexton's room. Grandmother held the lamp with one hand and my hand with the other. We glided down the hall in a disc of yellow light.

Captain Sexton's breathing was audible before we went inside. He opened his eyes, not seeing the light as much as sensing our presence. Putting the lantern on the nightstand, she put her hand on his forehead. "Cornelia," he rasped, "this ain't the end of it. This is just the eye. They's more to come yet."

Grandmother put her hand to her ear and reset her earpiece, thumbing the volume wheel in her pocket. "This batt'rey is dead. What'd he say, Becca?"

"It's the eye. There's more to come," I spelled, keeping my fingers in the light of the lamp.

"I know, Cap'n Sexton. I know. We're snug and we're ready for it."

"The back side'll be worse," he wheezed. He gestured toward his medicine. Grandmother put the digatalis in his mouth. I spelled, "The back side is worse." She nodded and felt for his pulse, sighing. Captain Sexton and I both heard the wind picking up. Grandmother knew it by watching us.

Captain Sexton put his cool, thin-skinned hand on my arm. "Little girl. Becca. Tell her I'm not going to make it through the night."

"He's going to die tonight," I spelled. The wind was shrieking now, accompanied by the sound of wood groaning and splintering. Captain Sexton shivered. Grandmother got him another blanket, but he shrugged it off, his milky blue eyes staring at the wall. His mouth moved, his jaw worked, but only a guttural sound emerged. He leaned back on the pillows again, limp. I could tell he was dead.

Grandmother tried to find a pulse in his wrist and then his neck. She took the mirror from my pinafore and held it under his nose. "He's gone," she honked. I nodded, refastening my mirror.

"Becca, what did he say?"

I tried to think how to spell it. "He said 'aargh,'" I spelled.

Grandmother blinked a couple of times, then swept me into her bosom, which would have been wonderful if her defunct hearing aid had been in a different pocket. She rocked me back and forth, shaking, the hearing aid crushing my cheek. She took me by the shoulders and held me into the light to see me better. "He said aaargh?'" I could see she was laughing. Adults could behave so strangely sometimes.

She turned and closed Mr. Sexton's eyes, then pulled the covers over his face. "It's going to be a long night, Becca. You're going to have to be my ears. Can you do that?" She wasn't laughing now. I nodded. She hugged me again, but this time I managed to get to one side of the hearing aid pocket.

We walked back to the lobby in the lamplight. The wind was screaming outside, awakening several of the old people. The glass doors to the dining room swung open and Beau motioned Grandmother to come. "Cornelia, bring the ones who are awake in here," he said.

"Her hearing aid battery's dead, Beau. So's Captain Sexton. I spell for her." I whispered it in his ear, but it must have been a juicy whisper because Beau shuddered a little.

"Girl," he said, "Tell her to bring the old folks who are awake in here. I've made some cocoa and warm milk." I spelled it for Grandmother. She nodded, motioning for me to tell the maids. They quickly brought in all those who were awake, without waking those who managed to sleep through the commotion.

Beau also had some oxtail soup with barley, mild and tasty. The old people felt better with something warm in their bellies. Those who began to drowse were taken back to the lobby to resume sleep. The maids were worn out.

"Becca," said Beau, "Tell your grandmother that the trustees and I will take charge now. The maids are going to be swamped tomorrow." I spelled it as best I could.

"Tell the maids, Becca," she said wearily.

"Go to sleep," I told them. "Beau's in charge."

Some of them almost dropped in their tracks with relief. A couple left for the inmate wing to look for beds with mattresses. I sat on a pillow beside Grandmother's chair and, leaning against her leg, fell asleep immediately. I woke once to the splintering sound of wood being ripped away from wood but went right back to sleep.

Dawn woke me, sitting beside the beveled panes of the big double doors that opened onto the porch. I was disoriented, trying to think why the piles of rope were on the porch. Then I realized they were moving!

I watched one snake in particular, a cottonmouth. Through the bevels it seemed hyphenated, broken, like a straw in a glass of water. Cottonmouths are grumpy in the best of times, and this one had struck at the glass so many times its venom was gone, streaked down the pane.

Snakes and other reptiles writhed in piles. Water stood within feet of the porch. Every square inch of lawn and shubbery not covered by water was covered with snakes, lizards, turtles, and small mammals. Not even horror movies ever showed me such a sight.

Grandmother's hand was on my shoulder. She had seen it, too. Waving me away, she collected pillows to stuff in the frames, obscuring the view. "It'll only upset people," she spelled, her hands shaking.

She and I tiptoed through the dining room. Beau and the trustees slept on blankets on the floor. Grandfather sat, asleep, with a shotgun between his knees in the colored dining room. I knew to approach a man with a gun slowly. "Grandfather." He opened his eyes and raised his head. Putting my mouth close to his ear I whispered, "Grandmother's battery's dead and so is Captain Sexton. He said 'aargh'. There's snakes hip deep all over the porch." He closed his eyes and sighed.

The water subsided as the hurricane roiled away. Grandfather gave strict orders for no one to go outside until the winds were completely still. I guessed it was not the wind that bothered him but the snakes. As much time as he spent in the swamp, he was wary of snakes.

Grandmother cleaned Captain Sexton up and put a decent suit of clothes on him. She and a couple of trustees lifted his thin old body and lashed it with a belt to a wheelchair. Early that morning, before the old people were awake, they tiptoed it through the hall and lobby and into the kitchen.

"Beau," she honked, "We haven't been friends a long time, but I think you know me well enough to know I'd never do anything to hurt a person's feelings." Beau looked puzzled. He already loved Cornelia Bass, though they had only known each other just a while. Adversity and danger draw people together quickly, but few promises are remembered when the wind is calm. Perhaps this old white lady had reverted.

"Captain Sexton died last night, Beau. I don't know when the undertaker'll get up here. I don't know when we'll get to bury him, but we can't let him stay in his room. Beau, we gotta...."

Beau was a sensitive man, despite his crime. Moved by her concern for his feelings, he could also see the humor and irony in the situation. He grinned; she was relieved. "We'll put him in the back and drape a tow sack over him. No one will even know he's there."

"Some of them know he's dead, Beau. You know they'll tease you...."

"Cornelia, I been teased all my life. For being big. For being black. For being queer. For being big and black and queer. This ain't nothin'. I can give 'em as good as I get. Don't you worry 'bout me, Miss Lady."

Grandmother patted his hand. "Thank you, Beau."

Grinning from ear to ear, the trustees rolled Captain Sexton into the ice house.

Four days passed before the guards' families got the mud out of their houses enough to move back with their cats and dogs. The prison farm lost about a quarter of its stock, but still had chickens.

The prisoners also slept in the main house for four days after the storm abated, cleaning mud and debris from the cells, noting that the water came almost to the ceiling of the cells on the bottom floor. There were a couple of brushes with snakes, both cottonmouths, both dispatched with a hoe. The prisoners salvaged mattresses and washed bedding. They scrubbed floors and walls. When they went up to eat they asked, "Beau, this ain't seafood, is it?"

After the prisoners and the guards' families had moved back, the undertaker came to get Captain Sexton, who by this time was stiff as a board.

Grandmother and the maids worked hard to get everything in order at the county home. In the commotion I lost the piece of yellow wood with the mirror, and the little bone and the feather from the sea harpy. Then I lost Aunt Martha. No feather, no bone or mirror could have saved me from the storms to come. I was helpless.

6

Somehow my father managed to find a house for us in Plimpton. Though it was just two miles from the Washington County Home for the Indigent that had been my home since I could remember, it might as well have been on the other side of the world. Grandmother was a world apart from me now. I hardly ever saw her again before she died.

Aunt Martha was now out of my world entirely, retreated back into the nether world of colored domestics, many of whom had lost their positions when the white women relinquished their jobs to returning soldiers and sailors.

The move from the Home to the Plimpton house also meant I had to leave my old and crazy playmates. No longer did I have the refuge of the Home after a day of runny-nosed kids and uncaring teachers.

No more the comfort of rump-sprung sofas or the thrill of high-backed wheelchairs. Our new house had the finest of post-war furniture from cousin Henry's store on the bypass. What he didn't carry he would get from Norfolk or Raleigh. Just point it out in a catalog or magazine, and Henry would find it. My father chose the furniture, of course, the way he chose everything. He directed us like characters in his play. We were his to use as he wanted.

Mother tried to assume the aura of mistress of the kitchen, but that was a facade. Father told her when to have the meals ready, what to cook, how to cook it and even where to buy the ingredients. Heaven help us all if the food wasn't to his liking.

By the time we moved to our new house, I was sleeping with my clothes on under my pajamas. It seemed to me that I never slept, although I must have. Many a time I awakened to find him over me in bed, his hands under my clothes.

He first raped me, actually penetrated me with his penis, when I was eleven. Sometimes when I am feeling especially strong, I try to remember the exact act, but I can't. I think it was the first time I had to really escape from my body to avoid the pain. Or perhaps I merely fainted.

I had whooping cough at the time, coughing until I lost my breath. He put his hand over my mouth. I was conscious of his being inside me, crushing my chest, tearing my vagina, stopping my breathing. I don't remember his withdrawing.

I do remember his being taunted by one of his brothers: "Why, you ain't nothin' but a little girl." My father socked him in the mouth, knocking him against a table.

I know now my uncle was kidding about my father's vasectomy. My mother wanted no more children. I guess I was part of the bargain. He was willing to give up his manly prowess, but only in return for what he wanted — me.

Reading became even more important. Though the main library seemed far away in the county seat, a bookmobile came to our little town and the school had a library of sorts. The bookmobile resembled a bread truck, and so did Miz Isa Marrow, the bookmobile driver. She measured exactly the same from shoulders to hips. I couldn't imagine that she ever had a waist.

She did have two children older than I. Her husband had been killed in the war. I remember when the thought of orphaned children brought a tear to my eye. That was before my father came home from the war. After that, I realized that orphans were the lucky ones.

Miz Isa Marrow must have been warned by Miz Simpson in the Plimpton library of my eclectic tastes in reading. When I checked out the thirty books allowed every two weeks she watched them like a hawk, quick to pluck any offending volume from the stack with a lecture on inappropriateness for my age.

Though she brought me books, I despised her, with her stringy, never-washed hair, cotton dresses straining at the seams and dingy around the neckline, and the sour smell she exuded. I wondered if she ever changed her underwear. She seldom changed the books on the bookmobile. Soon after I read my way through the age-appropriate books on the right hand side of the bookmobile, I made a fantastic discovery that I carried over into the rest of my life: Adults don't really know where anything is. They are almost always opportunistic, deadly to whatever is in their paths. Once the mass of objects in their responsibility exceeds their individual limit, the mass takes on a life of its own and takes care of itself.

Take Miz Isa. She had too many books to keep track of, so she solved that by changing them only every now and then — on the basis of volume, not quality. Too slovenly to even browse the main library for titles that might remotely interest her patrons, when the shelves were bare she'd back the bookmobile up to the library and grab a line of books between shoulder and waist high and near the door. So the bookmobile might have many books by authors with last names beginning with F through J, and another group from S to Z. She also had many books on botany; they must have been near the door, too.

I took advantage of her habits to start my book relocation program. Taking an age-appropriate book over to the other side of the bookmobile I'd pretend to be lost in thought. While Miz Isa complained to any other adult present, I'd slide the adult volumes I wanted out the louvered window she always kept open (she was going through the change and was always flushed).

So intent was she on her own affairs she never had an inkling of what I was doing. When I had checked out my thirty books I'd fly outside to pick up my adult volumes and mix them with my official stack. When I was finished with them I simply took them to the school library and put them back on the shelves. Miz Isa never noticed. The only thing that foiled my plan was rain. I could never bear to drop a book out in the rain.

The relocation project was a necessity. Reading was my only escape, and censorship was rampant. First the librarian decided which books were appropriate, then each teacher culled the motley lot again. Even Miss Hopkins, who considered herself a vestal of what culture existed in that town, augmenting her meager salary by giving piano lessons at her home after school, was not immune. The effect was deadening, especially to one who needed escape so desperately.

I read every waking moment. In class I always had a book in hand. Early on, I came to an unspoken understanding with each teacher: I would not raise hell and disrupt the class as long as I was reading. Their reward came at the end of the year. At achievement test time, my score would raise their class average.

At home at night, books were my drug. I read until time for bed, putting on my pajamas over my clothes, waiting for the adults to go to bed. As soon as I heard their door close, out came the goose neck lamp from my dresser and the extension cord from under my mattress. With both lamp and radio plugged into the extension cord, I retired to my closet, so they wouldn't notice any light showing from under the door. The earplug for the radio was so much like Grandmother's that I thought of her every time I listened to the radio.

Shortly after we moved to the new house Grandmother had a stroke. I visited her in the hospital, but she was no longer the same person. Even though she still wore her hearing aid, her deafness was beyond help. Even worse, the stroke took away her ability to talk with her fingers, nor could she read my fingers when I tried spelling to her.

The stroke also robbed her of that special ephemeral quality that made her so special, so apart from others. She didn't get like Mr. Coy Brown and cuss all the time. Grandmother seemed to develop edges. She became sharp and critical. When her neighbor, Ada, brought her strawberries, Grandmother pointed out that Ada knew that she had never liked the fruit and that it gave her a rash. She observed that Ada always tried to curry favor by doing trivial things for people, and that she had a positive attraction for the tawdry. Even the maids gulped at that little speech. Ada left in tears.

Grandmother started ordering Grandfather around, too. "Luther, we are going for a ride this afternoon," she'd say. "Have the car at the porch at 2:30." Grandfather would have the car there.

Another stroke six months later killed her instantly. I saw her body in the casket, looking too small, her hair frizzy, weird. The undertaker, Tommy Tucker, had applied her makeup with a broad brush. For the first time in her whole life, Grandmother wore nail polish.

In the funeral home I read everything I could find. Once I looked up to see Tommy Tucker's son (everyone called him "Little Tommy"), dressed in a suit and tie, standing with his father beside Grandmother's casket, the picture of decorum. Little Tommy, my age, was the only adopted child any of us knew. That, coupled with his father's occupation, made him both special and unapproachable.

Little Tommy grew up to go to embalming school, take over his father's business, marry his childhood sweetheart, father a child, and wear the finest clothes. Finally worn down by his wife's incessant haranguing to wash his hands before touching her, his food, or anything else, he climbed into a casket and blew his brains out with a hollow-point .22. Even then he went out in style, choosing a Willoughby, the Cadillac of caskets.

My grandmother's death made hardly a ripple in my life at the time. I miss her more now than I did when she died. Perhaps I was dead then. Who knows? I certainly didn't feel alive. Just as the corpse in the casket wasn't the Grandmother I had known, I wasn't the same person who had known Grandmother. We had both become something different. One of the things I learned early in the abuse was the cost of things. Christmas, school clothes, a dinner with no violence — all had a cost. The price was always the same. He took it from my body.

My first real job came during my thirteenth summer. He wouldn't let me have a paper route or work part time in the little store down the road. When I pressed him, the only work he'd allow me was field work. He thought I'd never do it. Within the week, I had a job chopping grass out of a neighbor's peanuts. All the grass-hoers were women. I was the only child in the group and the only white person.

The white man picked us up early, before the sun was up. We began chopping with dew still on the plants. By ten o'clock, the fields were a hell of heat. Humidity shimmered from the white earth, sandy and easy to work with the hoe.

At ten thirty, the white man brought ice water so cold it made the gallon jar sweat. The black women stood back, waiting for the white girl to drink first, but I was embarrassed. I said I wasn't thirsty. Scraping the thirst matter from my lips with my teeth I waited to drink from the pump under the tree where we ate our lunch.

After lunch, lulled by the black women's soft speech, I napped. It was the safest I had felt in years, since my Grandmother and Aunt Martha.

We worked eleven hours that day. We got paid in cash, $4.40. The next day, Saturday, I caught a ride into Plimpton with one of the fieldhands, my money in my pocket. I went straight to Leggatt's Jewelry Store, knowing exactly what I wanted. Mrs. Leggatt had it ready by the time I left town. I wear it to this day: A twenty-four-inch plain silver chain and silver disk with my name engraved on it. "Becca." If I had had my adult insight then, I would have known that I would make it. I would not die.

That was also the day I started saving money from my field work toward my escape. At first I kept it in an envelope in my top drawer, but I returned one evening to find the envelope in the middle of the floor, empty. He had taken almost twenty dollars.

When I inquired at the bank whether a child could open an account, they assured me I could as long as my parents filled out the paperwork. When I learned that this would give them access to the money, I realized I'd have to make other plans.

My father had a dugout canoe he kept down on the creek at the landing we called the Guinea Hole. The canoe had the utilitarian beauty of folksy, handcrafted articles, carved from a cypress tree in the old-fashioned manner: first the interior of the canoe was burned, then the charred wood was scooped out, finally it was burned again.

My father's attitude toward the things he owned was similar to the way he treated me. If he owned it, he could treat it as though it was worthless. He did that with the canoe. When he first brought it from Plimpton, he left it lashed to a boat trailer in the sun for three weeks rather than taking it directly to the water. When he finally launched it, it sank immediately, the wood split by the heat of the sun. Watching it sink, he stood on the bank cursing the black man who had so painstakingly carved the canoe. Someone was always to blame when things went wrong for him.

When I pulled the canoe up on a sand bar to bail it out, I discovered that the split in the bottom had swollen shut. I also found a paddle high and dry on the creek bank after a storm and hid it up in a tree.

The canoe was heavy and cumbersome on the bank, but in the creek it was a water sprite. One hard stroke of my paddle would send it shooting almost fifty feet across the water. Though I was the rankest of amateurs it seemed responsive to my every movement. Having read about the instability of canoes I decided to discover the limits of my craft. After standing, jumping and walking balanced along the gunwales, I learned that the information I had received from books covered Indian birchbark canoes not dugouts. It was stable as an aircraft carrier. Books also told me I was supposed to sit on the stern seat and paddle, but when I did, water oozed through the tiny split under my feet. When I sat on the bow seat the stern raised slightly and hardly any water came in.

In a matter of days I became a proficient paddler, able to make the canoe do my bidding, able to move over the dark waters of Kendricks Creek with no noise and hardly a ripple. Moving through the rich greens of the swamp, dappled with brilliant sunlight brought me solitude and security I needed during those years.

Increasingly I began to realize that what I read in books was important not just for escape or fantasy, but for practical reasons as well. That may have been self-evident for other children; for me it was not. For example, out of sheer boredom and because the slatternly Miz Isa Marrow had not changed the adult books in months, I started reading the botany section of the bookmobile's wares. I wasn't studying them; I read them exactly as if they were novels and for the same reason. Reading, the very act of reading, kept my mind going. Reading provided me a place to go. It kept me from thinking about what was happening to me.

I paddled along to the mill pond area where I usually turned the canoe around to go back to the landing. The mill had stood on a small hammock, its wheel turned by the current for years, until hurricane floods changed the flow of the river and took away the miller's living. The hammock had become an island, with one sizable cypress tree. Like most of the big baldies, it was hollow. About ten feet up from the buttress an opening, oval and smooth, was all but obscured by a vine.

I counted three leaves — poison ivy. I was disappointed, the hole in the tree being otherwise perfect for my need. When I looked closer, I recognized it was instead "rhus radicans Linnaeus," as I had remembered from the botany book, just what I was looking for.

As I beached the canoe and stepped onto the millstone, I looked around for the snakes I knew were there. A thump from my paddle on the millstone was answered by a watery plop on the other side of the big cypress. Was it was just a water snake? When I sensed no further movement I moved to the base of the big tree, searching again for anything that moved, paddle at the ready.

Feeling safer, I looked more closely at the vine. The stems were pinkish, with no prominent midrib on the leaf. It was definitely not poison ivy, but clematis. The silky pompoms covering the seeds told me I was right. I searched my memory for what I had read. Was it "virginianna" or "viorna?" I couldn't tell; it wasn't in flower. By the end of the summer the vine would obscure the hole. If I could just find a way to get up to that hole, the bald cypress would be my personal banker.

The next day I bought twenty of the biggest nails the hardware store carried. With my father's hammer I headed back to the mill pond. A Zesta cracker can held my money and a length of nylon net I had found on the creek bank.

After I had made sure no snake was close, I worked quickly to keep from feeling bad for scarring the tree, driving each nail halfway into it, hiding them behind the vine. When I reached the top of the nail ladder and found no wasps or bees inside, I hammered a final nail to the wood inside and dropped the hammer to the ground. Suspending the Zesta can in the pouch of the nylon net, I hung it on the nail, then climbed down to make sure it wasn't visible from the ground. I couldn't see the nails or the can of money in the tree. I felt like chortling. I felt another step closer to ...what?

Preoccupied, I didn't see the big cottonmouth on the bow of the dugout until I was on the millstone. Off-balance, I struck awkwardly with the blade of the paddle but hit only the wood beside it. The hammer fell from my hand, bouncing off the millstone and into the water. The big snake, its white mouth the size of my palm, struck at the hammer as it fell. When I slashed at it again, I managed to hit it a few inches up from the end of the tail. After it writhed out of the canoe and swam off, I found six inches of cottonmouth tail on the bottom of the dugout. I worried momentarily about losing my father's hammer but realized that he wouldn't miss one tool in the mess of his shop. I got back into the boat shaking like a leaf. I dreamed about snakes that night. It seemed that no place was safe anymore.

During that summer I made many trips to the old cypress to hide the money I made. By the middle of August, I had saved enough for school clothes and the radio I wanted. Then another obstacle greeted me at the landing where the canoe was tied. The painter had been replaced with a chain and lock. My father smirked at me over dinner that night. "If that's the way you want to play it...," I thought. The next day I bought an identical lock. When I could get to his keys I exchanged the new one for the one on his ring. The rest was easy, as long as I planned my trips carefully, sometimes slipping away from school, where no one ever missed me. He never realized the lock was changed.

My new Motorola could be played on batteries or house current. Its attraction for me was twofold: a directional antenna and an earplug. Devilishly expensive — almost $30 — it wiped out my savings in the Zesta can.

I hid the radio in the space under the bottom of my bottom drawer. At first the drawer squawked and balked when pulled out, but I followed the directions in a book of household hints, sanding down the runners and putting soap on the wood until the drawer moved smoothly and silently. Every night I readied my closet for a trip across the cosmos. In the yellow puddle of light from my gooseneck lamp my mind gulped down stories of rightful kings locked in towers of gloom, forced to endure a younger brother's horrid rule. Star-crossed lovers wandered toward each other on the heath, missing each other in the fog, captured by the mire.

In those volumes, people made monumental voyages for love and fortune. Women searched for lovers and children across raging torrents and over frozen wastes. Some remained by the hearth, repulsing would-be lovers, staying true to men who returned old, ragged and penniless. In truth, those stay-at-home books really didn't interest me that much. I identified more with the wandering men. I solved childish cases with Trixie Belden and the Hardy Boys and stole bread with Jean Valjean. Miss Marple and Hercule Poirot took me to England and the Continent. Jean LaFitte and Robinson Crusoe led me on searches for treasure. I scanned a watery horizon with the men of the Pequod for Moby Dick.

I read Shakespeare and Trixie Belden in the same month and with the same interest. Windswept islands, bloodstained hands and cackling witches, mad kings screaming at daughters all held my interest in the same way. They kept my mind busy and gradually I learned I could escape the swamp.

Through my earplug and the Motorola with the directional antenna came voices from magic places like Fort Wayne and Cincinnati. When the stations cranked up their power at night, I listened to WCKY, WOWO and WLS from Chicago. Their white-boy music buzzed in my ear as I read. I'd turn my directional antenna to pick them up clearly, learning names like The Amboy Dukes and Dion, realizing that the white boys were playing pablum compared to the black music I heard when unrecognizable stations warped into my radio occasionally. It was at the State Fair in Raleigh that I first really listened to music from black boys.

A sizable withdrawal from my Zesta can in the ninth grade bought my fare on the school's activity bus. We got on the bus early in the morning; it would take almost four hours on highway 64. Most of the riders, students mainly and their mothers, plus a couple of teachers, brought their lunches. Shoe boxes full of fried chicken cooked the night before were already sporting greasy circles on the cardboard. Biscuits, triangles of lemon pie with meringue full of gritty sugar, and oniony potato salad already crawling with salmonella filled other boxes on the luggage racks running the length of the bus.

I spotted Gwendolyn Chesson's parents as soon as I got on the bus. They were impossible to miss. Mrs. Chesson was surely the biggest woman I had ever seen, at least before I went to the fair. Standing almost six feet tall, just shy of four hundred pounds, grace was impossible for her. Walking she had to shove her mass from one hammy leg to the other. Her arms and legs looked shortened, fin-like. Because every movement caused exertion beyond the capacity of her lungs, she was almost always out of breath.

Mrs. Chesson spoke only occasionally, depending on a series of grunts and gestures to communicate her needs to Mr. Chesson. When sitting and able to breathe, Mrs. Chesson's idea of chatting was to string together dire warnings and judgments about people, ideas and things she knew nothing about.

Mr. Chesson was smaller than I, weighing not more than 115 pounds and hardly five feet tall. He skipped like a terrier around Mrs. Chesson as she ambled through life, opening her doors, bringing her pillows to make her more comfortable, dusting her huge body with baking soda in the summertime when she was prone to chafe and break out in heat rash. He seemed more her mahout than her husband.

Gwendolyn herself was a wan little thing, prone to stomach upset and head colds, with hair the color of her face. When she had to go outside for even a few moments, her hair would lighten to almost white, her face would become cherry red and her nose would run.

Gwendolyn's mother sat on one bus seat by herself and Gwendolyn and her father sat on the seat behind her. Mrs. Chesson warned us time and again about eating food at the fair. "I been to the fair in

Plimpton. Them fair folks is nasty. You don't know where they been. You don't know what's in that food."

I had money in my pocket and didn't give a damn if they served roast possum. I was starved for anything different. Pizza pie was high on my list; I'd heard about it on my Motorola, pizza pie with pepperoni, whatever that was. Mrs. Chesson could poke her face full of deviled eggs, but I was going to eat anything new and different the fair had to offer.

Under the grandstand a labyrinth of booths peddled repasts by women from the church guilds and fraternal orders of Raleigh. There was no way I could spend money with the Moose or the Shriners — they sold beer — and though quite lenient about who they considered to be eighteen, there was no way a ninth grader could pass. It didn't matter anyway. The church and civic groups featured pork barbeque, barbequed chicken, hot dogs and hamburgers, nothing to capture my interest.

I wandered out onto the fairgrounds. The rides were also about what I had expected, though larger and gaudier than any I had seen. My disappointment rose as I walked past hot dog stands. Then I saw the sign: "Pizza!" Was this the same as pizza pie, like on the radio? I stood back to read the menu. There were so many choices and combinations. I wanted to try them all, including the anchovies everyone in my books seemed to eschew.

Seeing something familiar is satisfying to someone young and unsure. I started with a slice of cheese pizza. The crust, dampish under the topping but puffed up and hard toward the edge, fascinated me. The only bread I had ever seen before was white store bread of the Wonder variety, dinner rolls made with yeast, fried corn pone, and biscuits. The smell of yeast in the pizza crust made it seem more familiar.

The cheese was also not familiar. Cheese had always meant cheddar, with only a few choices: mild for sandwiches for the weak of spirit; sharp for cheese lovers, by itself, scrambled into eggs, topping cheese toast, and in chunks in old people's coffee; and extra sharp for cheese straws, in biscuit dough and on mousetraps. The pizza cheese was almost white, with herbs I had never smelled before.

How to eat it? I watched other pizza pie eaters attack the slice from the pointed end, eating right through the damp crust, the white cheese stringing between the bite and the slice. I followed suit. The molten cheese blistered my soft palate, but the exotic taste and smell transformed the little saliva glands under my tongue into little fountains. Setting the slice down, I savored that first bite, trying to identify the flavors that bombarded my senses. Opinion seemed to be divided on eating the hard crust, but since some were doing it I tried it, chewing until it cut my gum.

My next slice was sausage pizza, pretty much the same as the first, with yeasty crust, white cheese, and herbs, but the sausage surprised me, sitting on top in little chunks, not links as I was used to. It was mild but flavored with an herb with a slight licorice taste. I ate the slice quickly, again leaving the hard crust.

The midway beckoned and I wandered toward it, mindful that the pizza pie stand would stay open for as long as I had my Zesta can funds. A man with a bulbous nose informed me and the folks standing nearby that we were just in time for another performance of the magic of the Dancing Waters. It would cost only a quarter, "one fourth of a dollar, cheap at any price" to hear the world's greatest music and view the magnificent waters inside. That sounded good to me. I paid and went inside the tent, choosing a seat in the middle of everything so I could see. Any seat in that tent would have had a view of the stage; I turned out to be the only viewer.

Quiet music began playing from what could have been only a juke box out of my sight. The music was fuller than any radio speaker I had ever heard, as full as if actual musicians were playing. A little hiss signaled the turning on of the Magic Waters, which began to rise and fall with the strains of what I later learned was Pachelbel's "Canon." The fountains and sprays swaying and surging to the music turned from clear and white to blues, violets and greens, so artful and poignant I felt tears in response.

Pachelbel faded in a minor tone into the air, leaving me breathless, hoping for more. More came with a change of the Magic Water colors from violet to light yellow, and from the sigh of violins to the siren's song of an oboe. The same musical passage was repeated and embellished by other instruments in the unseen, recorded orchestra, reminiscent of the children's game, Gossip: information passed from one to the next, until it got to the last child. Most of the time a kernel of the message would survive, but almost always the information would be altered.

This rendition of "Bolero" was like that game, each instrument making the music throb a little more. The waters in response became liquid fire of yellow, orange, and red. As the music pulsated and panted to crescendo, the movement of the fountains and lights became a holocaust. After the last of the brasses shrieked delight and the molten water jets became flaccid, I glanced around to see if anyone might object to such a spectacle being viewed by a child. Since I was still the only person in the tent, I relaxed for what was to come.

The next two numbers were silly even to my unsophisticated mind. "Margie" lilted and skipped, as did the Magic Water. "I'm Forever Blowing Bubbles" was predictable, bubbles rising from unseen blowers, drifting down from over now sedate fountains. My attention wandered to my surroundings, to be brought back with the crash of the finale.

Horns blared, cymbals clashed and piccolos giggled hysterically as the Magic Waters marched and cavorted through "The Stars and Stripes Forever." The air was filled with red, white, and blue light. I loved every moment of it. I left the tent, chest swelled with patriotism, whistling under my breath. It felt good to be an American and to have gotten my 25 cents' worth.

Late afternoon found me back at the pizza stand to sample again. The ground beef slice disappointed, with regular old hamburger on top, but I jazzed it up with some powdered cheese in a jar with holes in its metal top and some flakes of dried red peppers from a similar jar.

Anchovies are fish, I discovered. They lay on my slice of pizza pie like little brown commas, fishy and briny as spring herrings that poor people corned and ate for breakfast. Perhaps because of my familiarity with herrings, I enjoyed the anchovies. Stuffed with pizza

I wandered off toward the back part of the fairgrounds.

The arrival of evening had a profound effect on the inhabitants of the fairgrounds. Strapping farm boys from State College, stopping only for beer from the Masons' stall under the stadium, headed for the areas away from the midway, there to be joined by blond crewcuts wearing Weejun loafers, high-pocket pants and university fraternity pins. Preacher boys from Wake Forest and would-be ministers from Duke became one with the boys and middle-aged men from the outlying towns heading for the hootch shows.

A couple of girls with college boys seemed ashamed at being there. The only other females were a few young women with bleached hair, cutting their eyes at the boys from the university, and three middle-aged married women, nostrils flared, standing with their fat husbands.

Darkness magnified the light in the eyes of the barker extolling the virtues of the women on the outside stage, poised and occasionally pirouetting. They pranced up and down the platform as the barker promised sights beyond our fondest dreams inside the tent. The women went inside and so did most of the college boys. Those of us outside could hear the throbbing music and the whistles and jeers from the boys, until we moved on to the next stage and barker.

"Freaks!" the barker crowed from the next stage. From behind the tent flap came a woman with a beard and hair on her chest and legs, followed by a tall man and a tiny woman. "Inside," the barker confided to us, "is a woman so fat that she sweats blood." After my years at the County Home and after riding here from the swamp with Mrs. Chesson, I saw no reason to waste my money on things I'd already seen. It did occur to me to duck inside and tip the fat, blood-sweating woman to Mrs. Chesson's baking soda health tip, but I decided against it.

The light-skinned black man at the next microphone wasn't yelling. He didn't need to. Everyone leaned forward trying to block out any sound so as not to miss a word he said. His voice was honey, like his skin. As he crooned to us, light flashed and sparkled from the diamond embedded in the golden spade on his top right incisor. His powder blue satin tuxedo shimmered in the light, the golden thread in his dark blue cummerbund accenting his slender waist and hips. Every strand of his hair had been processed, highlighted with brilliantine.

Whispering into the microphone he invited hot poppas and chilly mommas to hear the music. Offering The Larks from Nashville, Blind Anthony on the piano, The Harlem Honeydippers and The Fatboys from Florida, he waved tickets for a dollar. Though it was as much as a slice of pizza, I was the first in line for the show.

That was the best dollar I ever spent. It changed my life. Blind Anthony played the piano and sang about Betty and DuPree:

"Betty told DuPree
I want a diamond ring."

It set the tone for the evening. White girls would never tell white boys what they wanted. White boys were supposed to know what white girls wanted, supposed to be born with the knowledge. Here was Blind Anthony singing about women driving men to drink and mayhem.

The Florida Fatboys sang a capella, except for a tambourine which the most corpulent of the porcine lot whacked on the most adipose area of his hip and thigh while the rest of the group clapped in time to the music. The Fatboys sang religious songs, though none that I had ever heard from the Missionary Society. They weren't spirituals, exactly; I'd heard most of those. These were about homes in the sky, to be sure, but sung with long wailing solo parts punctuated with frenetic backup singing. The lead Fatboy made that tambourine buzz like a rattlesnake. It was hard to keep one's feet from tapping.

The Harlem Honeydippers were worth the dollar by themselves. With a band composed of Blind Anthony, one of The Fatboys on sax and another on drums, and two guitarists from The Larks, The Honeydippers were five women of indeterminate age. Though two were very dark, all sported either red or blonde hair. One of the more light-skinned was almost fat enough to have sung with The Fatboys. Their gowns, which they changed three times, were outrageous in their colors and ability to remain together at the seams as The Honeydippers pranced and strutted. I had never seen people move that way, certainly not women. Their music pounded and pulsed, enveloping me with its intensity.

The Larks, on the other hand, were crooners. They moved in tandem and leaned forward, microphones in hand, singing to the women in the audience, singing of the loving they would provide, of cars and furs and of strutting through Harlem with the right woman on their arms. Slender men, The Larks wore matched satin outfits, like second skin on the buttocks and tight across the crotch. They oozed sensuality. More than one white man squirmed in his seat, pinching his butt together.

The finale was wonderful. The Larks and The Honeydippers coupled up. Blind Anthony tore up the piano, while The Fatboys trilled and boomed through three songs. I would have paid the rest of my pizza money for just one more. It was the first live music I'd ever heard, except for Miss Hopkins' piano.

Outside, the October sky was black as pitch. The lights of the midway obscured the stars. Small children had left with their mothers and the rides on the midway moved faster. Lights stabbed the darkness, pulsating and sharp, grabbing the eye, assaulting the brain. An urgency seemed to swirl. Many of the men had obviously stopped more than once at the beer stalls. The groups in front of the hooch shows were growing larger.

I wandered over to the box office at the stadium to see about the featured performance. The Radio City Music Hall Rockettes were headlined, along with a dog act, a chubby white male singer in a tuxedo, acrobats, and a group of older white males singing something called "barbershop." Looking at the line of families waiting to buy tickets, a restlessness rose up inside me. I didn't want to see white girls kick in unison. I didn't want to sit with families. I didn't want to spend the remainder of my money like that. Kicking happily back through the sawdust toward the tents with live music, freaks and hooch shows, I made a final stop at the pizza stand. I had saved the mushroom pizza for last. Since my father was highly allergic to mushrooms, they weren't allowed in the house. I bit the slice carefully. The mushrooms were sliced so thinly they assumed the flavor of the herbs and cheese. I waited to see if I would become deathly ill. When nothing happened, I ate the rest of the slice with gusto.

The lights and cacophony from the back of the midway didn't seem so sinister now. Perhaps the timbre had changed or I perceived it differently, but now the crowds in front of the little stages and the people on them seemed to know each other. Whistling and hooting, the men greeted the women. Everyone knew exactly what they would see out front and exactly what they would see inside.

The painted women stood with arms akimbo, kiminos open in front, snapping gum and grinning at the rubes. When signaled by the barker, a woman would walk a heel-dragging, stiff-legged walk up and down the stage, stopping to blow a kiss or bend over to expose her bosom, inflaming the group, making them more apt to spend seventy five cents on a ticket.

There were more than fifteen hootchy kootchy shows, each the same. Each had lovely girls, some of them virgins. Each promised ticket buyers sights that would change their sex lives and improve their marriages. I kept moving until I heard one barker refer to a woman as an Indian Princess. That got my interest. In the South, "Indian Princess" meant a light-skinned black woman a white man wanted to take to a motel. A lot of motels wouldn't allow blacks to rent rooms, but there were no such restrictions on Indians.

Princess Moonbeam was aptly named. Her lacy yellow peignoir accented her skin, light as a full moon. Silver stars adorned the tips of her bosoms and a child's toy headress on her head, the feathers also yellow. She was as bored as she could be. I moved on...unexpectedly to an adventure unfolding a side of the universe I never knew existed.

I walked in front of a group of ticket holders just as they surged into a tent, propelling me with them in their gusto. I tried half-heartedly to buck the tide, but when it was clear that I couldn't, I tried at least to make myself invisible beside a big timber at the side of the tent.

The women gyrated to the music, swinging hips and tasseled bosoms. Groups moved on and off the little stage as the women appeared with less and less on their bodies. They began soliciting dollar bills, moving up and down the aisles, inviting the men to thrust the money inside their costumes. Some of the scantily-clad, comely ones were absolutely festooned with cash when they went behind the curtains.

A fracas broke out when one of the men tried to retrieve money from one of the women's scanty briefs. Large men seemed to jump from shadows to grab the offender. Folding chairs flew and so did fists.

As I turned to run toward the door, I was caught by a shoulder or hip and thrust through the side of the tent, into the sawdust of the adjoining tent. Here men were shouting, cheering so loud they couldn't hear the fight next door. From my sawdust seat I saw I was myself next to Mr. Chesson and the shop teacher, Mr. Basinger, but they wouldn't have noticed me if I had landed in their laps. They were watching the woman on the stage insert a light bulb into her twat and turn it on!

Scooting backwards on my bottom toward the door, my progress was halted by a large footlocker and by the actions of the woman, who had by this time taken the 60-watter from her body and proceeded to smoke a cigarette with the same orifice. I was too stunned to move.

The smoker left the stage, replaced by a woman with absolutely nothing on her upper body except a halter painted on her ample bosom. The paint was purple. She danced and wiggled, leaving the stage to writhe up and down the aisles, staying just out of reach of the men.

Why is it that bald men, bearded men, fat men and small men seem to be lightning rods for teasing? The dancer with the painted breasts, spying Gwendolyn's diminutive father at the end of the aisle with Mr. Basinger, could not contain herself. Standing beside him she undulated and heaved, reaching with her hands to turn his face toward her. Mr. Chesson made some ineffectual tries at getting away, while Mr. Basinger kept punching him on the arm, laughing, the dancer grabbing him by his belt to pull him back to his seat. The rest of the men hooted. Egged on by their approval, she took his face in her hands and pulled him toward her bosom.

It was not a direct hit. Mr. Chesson managed to turn his face just in time, sparing the right side. Her right purple nipple caught him in the ear, the left one getting him just under his left eye. The whole left side of his face was greasy with purple paint. She reached for him again, trying to cram her ample breast into his mouth but, wiry and strong for his size, he pushed her into the crowd behind her and dashed for the door. It happened so fast I couldn't get my legs out of the aisle in time. He tripped over them, flying head first into the sawdust. I scooted back behind the trunk, but saw him stand up, the purple paint on his face covered in sawdust.

The force of the push or the hands of the men who caught her snapped one strand of her G-string, all she had on for a costume. In their zeal to get her back on stage by hoisting her over their heads, they snapped the remaining one. Back on stage as naked as a jaybird, arms opened wide she bowed to the adoring audience. Then she turned, spread her cheeks and expressed the esteem she felt for them in a trumpet call of flatulence, remarkable in intensity and duration.

Mr. Chesson missed the finale as he bounded from the tent, brushing the sawdust caked in the paint on his face with his hand, wiping it on his handerchief. Close behind him, I moved as fast as I could on my hands and knees to avoid his embarrassment at seeing me, finally hiding behind a knot of people.

With two dollars left in my pocket, I made a last pass at the pizza stand for the slices that would have to last me until the state fair next October. I ordered one with anchovies, the other with pepperoni. The very words were magic. Eating slowly, I felt as if my very brain had grown that day.

The food, the music, the dancing had changed my life, and I knew it. Even if the activity bus didn't come to the fair next year, I would find a way to get back here by myself.

Back at the activity bus, finding two tenth grade boys asleep on the back seat smelling of beer and its aftermath, I chose a seat just behind the driver, thinking about the possibility of never seeing the fair again. With my forehead propped on my hands on the chrome bar in front of my seat, I looked down and made another important discovery. There, at the side of the driver's seat, were maps. I pulled them out to examine them, maps of Virginia, the Southeastern United States, and one for North Carolina. All of a sudden I began to see possibilities.

Until now I had avoided riding in cars as much as I could, to avoid my father's sexual overtures. If alone, he would have his hands on me or under my clothes. Many times he had actually forced me to have sex with him in the car. I tried to deaden my mind by reading, merging myself into the stories even while it was happening. I was so on guard, so afraid or deadened to my surroundings I seldom even cared where I was.

The moment I saw the maps I realized the ramifications. The driver had followed the map to get to the fair. If I could read the map, I could get to the fair. If I could get to the fair by myself, I could get away!

I opened the North Carolina map. The light from the parking lot was dim, but I was used to dim light from reading in my closet. My heart stopped for a moment; the map seemed so complex! There were so many lines, and no indication of what the colors meant. Still I made myself study it. Suddenly I saw the outlines of the Sound and the small circle of Plimpton on the river. My finger followed route 64 until it came to Raleigh. It was as if map-reading revealed itself to me in an instant. Replacing the North Carolina map, I examined the one for the Southeast. There they were! Roads to Virginia, South Carolina, even Florida, all numbered, ready to be traveled. I could be free!

A whistle and a whump I felt in my chest signaled that the show was over in the stadium. The firecrackers woke the tenth graders, sending them outside to throw up again. Teachers, parents, exhausted children walked together to their vehicles. Mr. Chesson got on, sitting close to the window, pretending to go to sleep. He had managed to get the purple paint and sawdust off his face, but there was still a smudge on his collar. He ignored Mr. Basinger's smirk.

Tired as I was, I was determined to watch every move the driver made on the way home. I needed to know if I was going to escape. I watched as he eased the bus into traffic, choosing lanes, passing other vehicles. I watched for the NC 64 signs on the side of the pavement. I would have loved for him to talk out loud about his movements, but, as far as I could see, it wasn't that hard for an alert person.

About 25 miles out of Raleigh, near the town of Arno, still heading east on 64, we heard strange sounds coming from Mr. Chesson, loud enough to wake Mr. Basinger, who bounded up the aisle to where Mr. Chesson and Gwendolyn were sitting. He directed the driver to pull into a service station whose lights shone in the distance. In that short time, Mr. Chesson's distress had grown.

Green mucous bubbles were forming at the left corner of his mouth. His ear, even in the 12-volt dome light of the bus, was red as a beet, puffy and thick like a catcher's mitt. Under his left eye red blotches pulsated. The corner of his left eye began to draw downward toward the corner of his mouth.

Mr. Basinger and the driver lay the stricken man on his back on the floor and Mr. Basinger bolted for the service station. I heard adults say "stroke" and "heart attack," but it was unlike any seizure I had ever seen. If anything, it reminded me of the reactions of people Aunt Martha read the roots on, but I kept that to myself. People don't like to hear children talk about such things.

Mr. Basinger jumped up the steps of the bus and panted out directions to Arno's hospital. The emergency crew was expecting us. The parallel education I had begun at the fair was not over; I settled back, determined to absorb every single thing I saw.

Children and adults passed their jackets to the front to cover Mr. Chesson and make him more comfortable. Poor Mrs. Chesson, rendered breathless by Mr. Chesson's condition and unable because of her bulk to tend to him, sat like a land-locked pinniped, barking out single words and bits of phrases, making choppy, unintelligible gestures with her hands. Gwendolyn, pale as paste, sat sobbing and shuddering on the seat by herself.

The bus driver came to a gravel-scattering halt beside the emergency door of the squat flat-topped brick hospital. Popping the door open, he and Mr. Basinger helped the orderlies load the little man onto the gurney. Mr. Basinger, the bus driver, Mrs. Chesson and

113

Gwendolyn followed the gurney inside, leaving the rest of us in the bus with its engine running and the door open. As I reached for the handle to close the door, one of the adults said, "Let's go into the waiting room where it's warm."

We did. The whole busload of us went through the swinging emergency room doors toward the waiting room, each retrieving his jacket as we passed the pile that had been warming Mr. Chesson. Since some were hungry from the day at the fair and the new excitement, those with food left in their shoe boxes brought them. Before leaving the bus I reached over and got Mrs. Chesson's boxes, knowing she would never let Mr. Chesson eat hospital food.

The whole busload of us tiptoed through the halls of the hospital, as quietly as we could, following the arrows to the waiting room. I spied Mrs. Chesson in the hall with a nurse. The nurse was talking, while Mrs. Chesson stood panting and listening. A polite child, I stood back, waiting until the conversation was over to give Mrs. Chesson her food.

The nurse put her hand on Mrs. Chesson's mammoth arm and said, "...he's from a country north of India, but he studied in England and this country. He's a psychiatrist at Dorothea Dix during the day, but he works the ER here at night. We're very lucky to have him here in this little hospital."

As young as I was, I could sense craziness brewing. Dorothea Dix was known in the vernacular as Dix Hill, The Loonie Bin, The Funny Farm, The Laughing Academy. It was the mental hospital for crazy white folks in the eastern part of the state. I shrank against the wall, to make myself inconspicuous. I knew he was the doctor when I saw the white coat and stethoscope around his neck. He was also wearing a turban. If I had been a member of the Free Will Baptist Church, I would have shouted, "Thank you, Jesus." I was delighted to be privy to such drama on the horizon.

The turbaned doctor, with his dusky skin and eyes like a fawn's, extended his hand. "Madame? Mrs. Chesson?" he said. He sounded like a high-toned Negro from New York or an English gentleman. Mrs. Chesson made a sound like an old roof giving way or a big limb splitting from a tree. It was the sound of the resolution of great strain

I was glad to be standing out of the way. The doctor had to scramble. Mrs. Chesson's legs retracted beneath her skirt and her huge body lurched against the wall, hit the floor, and rolled onto her massive stomach.

Orderlies and nurses gathered quickly, standing around the edge of her, unable to decide what to do first. The doctor was very calm. "Perhaps we should have two gurneys," he said. They were brought and placed side by side, fastened together with adhesive tape. "It is providential that she settled on her stomach. We can roll her onto the gurneys," directed the physician. Still Mrs. Chesson was a load, and it was hard to get her off the floor. They rolled the tethered gurneys with their heavy cargo toward an empty room.

By this time revived, Mrs. Chesson began thrashing around, moaning. "He's a nigra!" she wailed. "Don' let that nigra in that do-rag touch me. Don' let that nigra in that do-rag touch me."

The doctor gestured to a nurse with a hypodermic needle, but another nurse said, "Doctor, not now. Maybe she can help get herself onto the bed if she's awake."

The doctor nodded and the procession continued down the hall into a patient room, Mrs. Chesson moaning every moment. I stood outside the door, clutching the boxes of food, listening to every word. It sounded as if the doctor was directing the examination. Mrs. Chesson's moans became quieter, then stopped. I could hear her labored breathing in the hall.

Orderlies and nurses began leaving the room. Suddenly the doctor stood before me. I wanted to apologize to him for Mrs. Chesson's mean words, let him know that not everyone from my town would have felt that way, but both of us would have known that it was a lie. As I stared at him, a word I had read in books but had never used in conversation leapt into my mouth, "Xenophobe."

"I beg your pardon?" he said.

"Xenophobe. Both of them are."

"Are you the daughter, little girl?"

"No. I'm Becca. I went to the fair, too. Their daughter's Gwendolyn."

He nodded. "What's in the boxes, Becca?"

"Their food."

"They packed their lunches?"

"All of them did."

"Where is your box, Becca?"

I looked into those wonderful, liquid eyes and grinned. "I don't have a box. I eat pizza." I said it proudly.

He grinned back. "I see," he said. He took the boxes from me and seemed surprised by their weight. "What's in here, Becca?"

"Oh, fried chicken, deviled eggs, slices of lemon pie. Stuff like that."

He nodded. "It was very perceptive of you to think that the lunches they packed would make them feel more at home here. Thank you, Becca." I nodded back, embarrassed, unable to speak.

He handed them in to a nurse. "Lunch," he told her.

"Do you have any idea of what happened to the Chessons today, Becca?" The question came out of the blue. It caught me off guard. I chewed my lip and looked around quickly.

He stopped and held up a forefinger. Tapping on a door and receiving no answer, he went inside and turned on the light, then waved for me to follow. My hair must have stood on end. I was very cautious of rooms with beds. In a flash I realized that this man would probably think I thought he was a nigra in a do-rag if I didn't go inside. The fear of the man in a room with a bed made me hesitate. The rational part of my brain shouted that I had nothing to fear, but the survival instinct is great. I went just inside and stood in front of the open door.

"What happened, Becca?"

"What happened?" I felt my mind clouding over. All I could see was the bed. What was this man talking about? What did he mean, 'what happened'? What happened when? What happened where? I couldn't focus. I leaned on the doorjam, concentrating on the doorjam across from me.

"What happened to the Chessons?"

As I concentrated on the doorjam, my mind became sharper. "They are from the country. This trip upset them," I was able to mumble.

"But Becca, Mrs. Chesson fainted and Mr. Chesson's face is

swollen. Do you know what happened?"

I nodded, trying to think how to tell this person while not incriminating myself in the process. Children aren't supposed to go to hootchy kootchy shows.

"Becca," he said in a gentler voice, "if there is anything you can tell us, anything, we'd really appreciate it. Both of these people are in a bad way. If we don't have direction, if we don't know where to start, we'll have to do a battery of tests..."

"OK, OK." I felt safer and could think better. "I was over at the back on the fair, back where all the shows are." I glanced at him to see if he suspected what I was talking about. He nodded. "I was kind of standing in a group of people who went into a hootchy kootchy show...." I wondered if he knew what that meant. "That's a show where women dance...." He nodded. "I kind of went inside with them. A bad fight broke out and I got knocked through the side of the tent." He didn't seem a bit surprised by anything so far. "I rolled into another tent and I was right beside Mr. Chesson and Mr. Basinger."

"They didn't see you?"

I couldn't help grinning at that question, and it helped loosen the knot that had formed inside my chest. "No," I told him and chuckled.

"I see. I take it that it was not a tent in which educational programs were presented. They were attending to more pressing matters?"

That made me laugh. "They were watching women dancing." I decided not to burden him with the details. He would know, I was sure. "There was one woman, she didn't have a top on. She had a halter painted on." He nodded again.

"Purple."

"Purple?"

"The paint on her....ah, bosoms was purple."

"I see."

"She got some of the paint on Mr. Chesson's face." I waited a moment and saw that he understood. "She got it in his ear and almost got some in his eye. It was all over the side of his face. He tripped as he ran out and sawdust kind of got into the paint, too. The next time I saw him he had wiped most of it off, except for some on his shirt collar."

As casually as I could, I wandered out into the hall. Relief at being outside the room, at having the story out, made me giddy. The doctor with the turban followed me. He held out his hand for me to shake. "Thank you for your help, Becca. It will save us much time. Now, perhaps you can introduce me to..."

"Gwendolyn?"

"To Gwendolyn." We walked down the hall and into the waiting room. It looked like the Wreck of the Hesperus. Students and adults had made themselves at home, sprawled all over the chairs, chair arms and tables. With soft drinks from the machines they had started on the remainder of their food. Most of them, students and adults alike, were smoking. Waxed paper from chicken and sandwiches was everywhere. I was ashamed of them.

The whole group stopped in mid-bite when the doctor entered the room. He was exactly as Mr. Basinger had described to them. Gwendolyn handed her sandwich to the person beside her and started whimpering.

"Mr. Basinger. Gwendolyn." The doctor motioned toward the door.

The Chessons did not continue on the bus with us, but stayed in the Arno hospital for two more nights. Gwendolyn stayed at her grandmother's house. After all that excitement I doubted if we would ever go to the fair again, but we did. We went every year.

7

After the excitement of the State Fair and the possibilities it showed me, school became even more meaningless, like the caution light that hung above the intersection of Main and Boush streets. Years ago it had flashed yellow on Main and red on Boush. After someone shot out the lenses and bulb, it served only as a home for mockingbirds to raise their broods.

The light wasn't needed any more. A bypass had been built to direct traffic toward the beach and the Sound bridge, and the town began its unconscious glide toward oblivion, pulling in on itself like the face on an apple doll. Like an old scar, it puckered and pulled, getting smaller and rattier and more frayed as each teenager, diploma in hand, fled the town for Plimpton and beyond.

School seemed to exist only because of state laws. For example, Mr. Basinger, the agriculture and shop teacher, every two years was forced into teaching civics. It was there I was first introduced to blatant racism. Incensed by demands of "uppity nigras" he had read about in the *News and Observer*, Mr. Basinger passed around a mimeographed page with a picture of a black man on the left and a gorilla on the right. Beside each was listed the physical attributes of each. Not surprisingly, they were the same for each.

Even though I was only in the tenth grade, even though the only time I ever left that swampy county was to go to the state fair, even though the hell of my family life was forcing me back into myself, I knew those pictures were the product of a diseased and hateful mind. No one in my books used words like that. No one on the radio said things like that. The irony of seeing that level of race hatred in a civics class was lost on me until I remembered it as an adult.

Mr. Raymond Skyles taught math, both regular arithmetic and algebra. Except for his odd fascination for things numerical, he seemed like a nice enough man. His clothes were nicer than other teachers, and he never folded up his sleeves the way most of the men in town did. When Sharon Beasley, whom the boys called "Sharon, share alike," had her miscarriage in General Math class, Mr. Skyles calmly directed us into the auditorium and dispatched one of the boys to get Mr. Basinger. Wrapping her in a sheet and blanket from the sick room, they carried her down the stairs in a straight-backed chair to Mr. Skyles' Buick for the drive to the hospital. He was always nice to students, including Sharon, who, as far as I know, never conceived again.

Miz Neva Bailey taught Home Economics but every two years she had to teach chemistry and biology. To ease her phlebitis she wore a stocking-like elastic legging that started above her knee and extended over her foot, with holes cut out for knee, heel and toe. Since she was plump, flesh pooched out of the holes, looking for all the world like gigantic jelly beans. Some days she added a long Ace bandage held closed by a little metal device resembling a butterfly with teeth. She wrapped the bandage around the bum leg a couple of times a day, elevating the offending member whenever she could. From Miz Bailey I learned that cocoa and brown sugar should be packed to be measured. One's progress down the path of life is limited if one depends too much on one's skills and knowledge of measuring. In chemistry she taught me to pronounce "molecule" mo-lec'-u-al.

I took four years of typing but never got over 17 words per minute. I'd find myself reading the material and my fingers would stop moving. Typing was taught by Miz Jasper, a nice young woman just out of college. Even though she wasn't much older than her students, she wore old lady shoes. She also taught shorthand, which put her even further across the chasm into the adult camp.

English was my only interesting class, but even here I was so far ahead of the others it was a struggle to keep interested. English was the domain of Miz Lewis, who also taught French. When she discovered me in the library reading the dictionary and realized my interest and thirst, she opened her personal library to me.

Although I had had a couple of violent headaches earlier, when I was fourteen they descended on me with regularity, making my head throb in a hell of pain and my vision blur. My whole body would cringe at the slightest sound or movement. Nausea wracked me with such force that I ate just to have something to ward off the dry heaves.

At first, when a migraine started, I would lie in my darkened bedroom, moving only to throw up, until it waned. Sooner or later it would ease off and leave, but it might take as long as thirty six hours. As much as I wanted to keep my headaches secret from my mother, it was impossible. I heard her tell a neighbor that they were caused by excessive reading in poor light. She threatened to limit my reading severely if the headaches continued.

During that godawful year, she also showed her intense concern for my welfare when one of my periods wouldn't stop, wearing on for ten days and then fourteen. She asked me if I had been "messing around" with boys. If the bleeding didn't stop, she would take me to the doctor to examine me "down there." Her maternal instincts were not as strong as her need to avoid any trouble, especially trouble that could come to the attention of my father.

Though I hated her for her threats and insinuations, I was sure that I was indeed the cause of the extended bleeding and the violent migraines. Her words about my reading in poor light and her threat of setting limits on my reading kept returning to my mind. Taking the crisp paper from the Blue Diamond and sliding the folded cardboard sheath from the sharp side, I made my first suicide attempt. She found me and bound my wrists, then scrubbed the stains from the grout in the tile. She never asked me what was wrong or took me to the doctor; never, not even after other attempts later. Her fear of her husband was as great as mine.

I retreated deeper into the darkness of pretense and denial, making sure I did nothing to call attention to myself, blending in with the other students in school, acting as though nothing was wrong when a migraine swirled and pounded. Whenever the pain became intolerable and it seemed certain I would never get away, I'd try to kill myself.

A new principal arrived. Short and round, standing no more than five feet tall and almost bald, Mr. Smythe looked like the inflatable child's toy which pops up when it's been punched. His wife was similarly shaped, though smaller. Standing together they resembled salt and pepper shakers. Their hands were like pitty-pat squashes, thicker than wide, with short, stubby little fingers.

Misshapen hands didn't keep Mr. Smythe from feeling up the girls. With those whose families had some status in the community, he would merely slide his arm around their waists and walk down the hall talking cheerily. With those of us from the swamp, with those known as "loose as ashes," or with girls who had been in trouble at school, he was more direct, his fat little hand lingering on a hip or sliding down a buttock. His most disgusting habit with us low-status types was to snap our bra straps as we walked by.

The first time he did it to me as I walked out of his office, I went nuts. I hit him on the sternum with my shoulder, trying to knock him down. I called him a son of a bitch. I told him I'd kill him if he ever touched me again. After a period of silent staring, he sat back down in the plastic-covered chair that dwarfed him, then chilled me by asking calmly, "Tell me, Becca, just where do you go on that boat?"

Though just fifteen, I was well schooled in the hidden intentions of words and phrases. I'd been hyperalert for years, studying every facet of information, verbal and otherwise, proffered by any adult. Young and helpless, what I didn't know was that the fat little man was playing his trump card. He was trying to make me fearful. It would never work with an adult woman who knew her rights. No woman with hair under her arms or stubble on her legs, no strong person would ever have to worry in his presence. He preyed on the young and fearful. He abused his position.

His question made my head spin and my hands shake. He had seen me slipping away from school toward the Guinea Hole. Though I tried to look defiant, glaring at him, his tactic worked. I was afraid. "Where I go is absolutely none of your business," I said. Even to me it sounded weak.

"I just think I'll put a little kink in your wandering ways," he said.

I could feel the panic rising. "I'm going to tell Miz Jasper what you did." In my terror I watched his every twitch and movement.

He seemed to ignore me, picking up a stack of papers to thumb through. He glanced up from his papers. "Get out of my office," he said.

I continued my trips from the Guinea Hole to the cypress where I hid my money. Though I tried to be careful sneaking away from school, I know he saw me a couple of times, but he never again accosted me about it.

School had been a haven in my life, a refuge away from home, a hiding place where I could read whole-heartedly with all my attention. Mr. Smythe's bra-snapping ways altered that. At home I guarded against my father as much as I could. On the hammock with my cypress bank I walked guardedly because of the truncated water moccasin that was always there, that I saw almost every trip. Trying to make the situation lighter, I named the chopped-off snake "Bob" and tried to imagine him dressed up in a three-piece suit like a banker, but I was very careful.

Danger was omnipresent. I was always on guard. When I allowed myself to be distracted or my alertness failed me, I found my father on top of me at night, caught Mr. Smythe watching me in the hall, or realized that the bobtailed snake was too close. I knew I'd have to be more careful. I knew it was my fault that misfortune befell me. Those were the times I thought of the Blue Diamond with longing. Yet knowing I could kill myself gave me the courage to keep on living, to keep on trying to get old enough to leave.

Everything I read or heard on the radio told me how out of the mainstream my life was. Music that I loved I heard only on radio from other places, never in the town. In books people ate pizza and bagels with cream cheese and lived in places with subways and buses and traffic jams.

As the blacks in the rest of the country began to demand their rights, the South itself, once so comforting to me, became more menacing and mean-spirited. I became determined to leave it all, including my accent.

Miz Lewis, the French and English teacher who had offered me her own books, brought a magazine from France to school one day. Not having a penchant for languages, I couldn't read much of it, but I was fascinated with the pictures. Every detail was a revelation: They had houses! They had cars and boats! The pictures of people and places made me feel like I did at the state fair. France was attainable, within my reach. Things there were recognizable, manageable.

In one advertisement girls my age were wearing all black clothing. Black shoes, black stockings. Some even had on black lipstick. I knew immediately this was for me. These girls standing with thin-lipped, pouting boys, or riding on the backs of motorcycles made my heart lurch. I wanted to look just like them.

Laura Lee Saxton set the fashion tone in the high school, however. Her aunt owned a dress shop in town. When she bought for the shop, she bought for Laura Lee. Destiny's darling, Laura Lee stood five feet three inches tall, with reddish blonde hair and dark brown eyes. Lithe, athletic and thin, in the summertime her hair became even more blond as she tanned wonderfully. Laura Lee had all the clothes in the world, wearing outfits with flats to match when the rest of us wore dopey plaid dresses and saddle shoes. She never wore socks with her loafers.

Her aunt bought the top of the line for her: Jonathan Logan dresses with cummerbunds emphasizing her tiny waist, puffy skirts stuffed with starched and pressed crinoline to make her legs look thinner, Jantzen bathing suits and sports clothes with the diving woman label clearly visible. Best of all were the flats in every color Capezio ever made. The thin little soles and heels glorified her thin little feet, their leather as soft as butter, their colors like Easter eggs and jewels. Laura Lee had so many clothes she often returned after lunch with another stunning matched outfit with shoes to match, each outfit again perfect on her slight, 83 pound frame.

The words "anorexia nervosa" were not yet in our vocabulary, but even if they had been, most of us would have still been jealous of Laura Lee. Everything she wore was lovely and stylish.

Laura Lee lasted only one quarter in college, a large school with many stylish women, no one noticing or caring that she changed outfits between classes. She came home quietly to marry the son of a well-to-do farmer, who built her a brick ranch house with a white sofa. They adopted two children; Laura Lee never had her period, not even once. Every year they vacation by driving their new Chevrolet to Indianapolis for the 500 Mile Race.

I had no idea how to get that black clothing in the French magazine, but I was determined to try. Black sweaters with folded down collars and black skirts were easy enough. I made a major trip to the Zesta can for a pair of black Capezio flats, real ones, not a cheap copy from Butlers.

The clothes and shoes stayed hidden in the back of my closet while I scanned *Seventeen* and *Glamour* magazines in the school library for black stockings to complete the French magazine look, but they eluded me. Finally in an article about dancing I realized that the article of clothing I wanted was called "tights." Finding it was easier once I knew what to call it. Black nail polish and lipstick were available, too, but my nails were chewed to the quick and I didn't wear much makeup of any color. I loved my black clothing. Miz Lewis, who must have seen the ad with the French girls and their pouty boy friends, said she liked my clothes.

Racist Mr. Basinger said ominously that I looked like a beatnik, and asked if I was one. I assumed he meant some kind of religion like Catholic or Baptist and said no. Beatnik was not in any of our dictionaries. Only when I stumbled upon Miz Lewis' copy of "On the Road" by Jack Kerouac did I realize the implications of being called a beatnik.

I took Kerouac's words with a grain of salt after I tried smoking tea. There were no cigarette papers around, so I used the paper from the tea bag to roll a crude cigarette. My ineptitude made it quite a messy operation. The Lipton kept sifting out of each and wouldn't stay lit, no matter how I tried. The beatnik life would have to bump along without me, but I still loved my black clothes.

A golden opportunity appeared in the form of a school bus driving course, a plum of a job usually reserved for boys, since everyone understood they needed money more than girls and because of their superior driving skills and mechanical dexterity. We girls were allowed this wonderful opportunity thanks to happenings on the other side of the world.

For one thing, the Godless Russian Communists launched Sputnik, proving that our second-rate educational system was lagging even further behind. The search for talented high school graduates forced colleges to expand to accommodate more of the baby boomers looming like a tsunami on the shores of academia.

About the same time, the Suez Crisis spurred a large number of boys to sign for the military because of the alert. Every boy in our class except one enlisted. It was like World War II in microcosm. The men marched away and the women filled in to do the work.

Whenever I think how monumental world events impact the lives of the common person, I immediately think of the Suez Crisis and how I got college money. Somebody had to drive the school buses. The one boy left in our class got one of the slots, of course, but I was one of four girls chosen as drivers.

Another surprise awaited us in bus driver's class: The instructor was a woman. She was a good teacher, well spoken and an excellent driver, putting us through our paces in the classroom as well as in the school bus. At the end of the two week course, the scores showed that Melvin, the only boy in our class of eleven, just made it. All the others were girls.

I was given Bus 44. My route went down the beach road to pick up the Dorsey children at the end, then down the Comber lane to get eight more families. I drove down the New Farm Road for about eight miles to the Gospel Light Free Will Baptist Church, then back along the Jasmine Spit Road, past beach cottages and the casino where fast local girls danced the night away with Marines from across the Sound, and back to school with a full load.

I drove the route the first day with the emergency brake on, my wheels smoking by the time I got to school. Sure I'd lose my license, I told the mechanic what I had done. He didn't seem surprised and had it fixed before that afternoon's route.

Getting the school bus was a real turning point. Besides giving me an opportunity to escape to college, I found that I really liked the kids on the bus. They were a lot younger than I and seemed to think I was a goddess. That was nice, a first for me. I responded by trying to be fair and kind. Good-natured chatter was OK, but not rowdiness. Every child got a turn at "running the tracks," the coveted task of checking railroad tracks from both ways before waving the bus across. For most drivers that was a patronage position to hand out to favorites, but my kids liked knowing that everyone would get a turn.

I kept my bus spotless, washing it twice a week, more if needed, and sweeping it every afternoon. The Dorsey kids, first on the bus in the morning and the last off, closed all the windows before they left the bus in the afternoon. I paid them a quarter every payday, making them the envy of the other children. Every payday I left school at lunch time and walked to the bank to cash my check. Out of $86.67, each month I kept $6.67 to spend on myself and took $80 in twenties to the Zesta can. College was getting closer.

At the end of my junior year I scored in the top ten percentile in the state on the pre-SAT. It wasn't that hard. All my reading really helped.

Grass-filled acres of peanuts and soy beans put money in my pocket in the summers and kept me on the creek to the press tree. I worked the white earth of neighbors' fields, in the chill of dawn watching the magenta sun glide to zenith, lightening in color, warming the land at the end of my hoe. By ten o'clock the sun was white. Forms of other workers wavered in the distant heat. Man-made structures, barns and outhouses, wiggled as if made of gelatin. The white sun and white land sucked the color out of everything. Red headscarves, a bright blue shirt, dark brown skin, all faded in the intense light and heat.

Heat and light and long days were compelling to the crops, if not to us. We'd start chopping early in the day, working the blades of our hoes in the sandy soil, sliding them under the surface, feeling for the roots of the weeds and tussocks instead of merely cutting off the crown growth.

Working the fields approached Zen. Though we kept pretty much in a group as we moved along the rows, each of us was isolated in her thoughts. Eyes seemed to be attached to hands and arms, bypassing the brain, leaving it to think the thoughts that would make the enormity of the field more manageable. I have no idea what the other women thought about in their cocoons, protecting them against mind-numbing, repetitive movement, against light that sucked all color, heat that sapped all energy and the knowledge that work done today would be obliterated tomorrow by ubiquitous encroaching vegetation.

I accepted the return of the grass, the length of the rows, the enormity of the fields. I chopped at the tussock just ahead, the weed already topping the crop. Within myself I moved alone through the intensity of the heat and light, thinking about Cleveland, Pittsburg and other magical places, surprised by the end of the row, by lunchtime, by knock-off time. I could read what was inside my mind.

Working in tobacco made more money for the Zesta can, but cost some of the blessed privacy of fieldwork, since the work was done in a more social setting.

Tobacco season started with priming the sandlugs, removing the early-maturing smallish leaves growing nearest to the ground which were used for trash products like snuff. Since tobacco ripened from the bottom of the plant to the top, sandlugs were harvested first.

Everyone hated sandlugs. The primers, young men and strapping teenage boys had to bend over to snap off the leaves, holding them in bundles or sheaves under their arms as they moved down the rows. Because the sun dried the top leaves of the tobacco first, the primers would be dripping with dew until afternoon. The sandy soil coated the bottom leaves, sticking to the dewy surface and the resin in the sandlugs, then transferred in the handling to the clothing and bodies of the primers. They quickly became wet and dirty. The weight of the sheaves, the physical condition of the primers, most relatively inactive since the last harvest season, and the continual bending and straightening did not improve their disposition.

Primers loaded the leaf onto wooden carts the width of a mule. Tow sacks opened along the selvage served as sides for the cart. The mule moved along the rows, finally dragging the loaded carts to a shaded area under a big tree or to a barn porch where the barn crew worked. Women both black and white made up the barn crews. The white ones were usually young like myself, often still in high school. The black women were older.

Handers picked up the leaves in bundles of three or four leaves, more if they were sandlugs. Straightening the stems to even the ends and facing the leaves in the same direction, they handed the bundles to the tier.

Tying was a good job. A good tier made almost as much money as a primer. Having placed a tobacco stick into the notches of the wooden tying rack, she would tether the string from the cone on one end of the rack, her hands flying. It took at least two handers to keep even a mediocre tier busy.

The tiers seemed cut from the same cloth: thin, nervous black women tending toward hyperactivity. Good tiers with fast hands and mouths to keep the handers hopping were at a premium. They commanded more respect than most of the primers and were the only hands who didn't have to help barn the tobacco at the end of the day.

Primers climbed the cross members inside the barn and, starting from the top, hung the sticks heavy with tied leaf on the racks.

At one time the crop in the barn was cured with wood. Many a young farmer and his wife slept in the barn or its shelter during wood curing season. The hands made jokes about who was conceived in which barn. Much of the banter was true; many children from the Costal Plain were born in March, April and May. The jokes were about farmers who would stoke the fires and then their wives.

Cheap oil allowed the wood stoves to be replaced by oil burners by the time I worked tobacco. Timers, switches, and pilot lights made it possible for the farmer and his wife to sleep inside their homes through the summer.

By the end of the sandlug days the rhythm of the work created a momentum that carried us all along. Tiers had favorite handers who positioned each hand just so. Barn hands flew through a cart so fast there would be only a few minutes of respite between carts.

Primers, by now in better condition, removed the larger, easier leaves up the stalk. Cart drivers made sly remarks about the barn crew spending most of the day standing around waiting for work. The primers would almost kill themselves to get a cart or two ahead before lunch time, to make their job a little easier in the afternoon heat.

The hands would work until the fields were finished. We were disgruntled if we didn't get a day's work, and many a time we worked past summer dark to get the barn in. Covered with sticky brown resin from the plant and gritty white sand, we'd drag our weary bodies home, almost too tired to bathe and prepare for the next day.

I was usually in school when most of the grading of the tobacco leaves took place after the tobacco was cured, but I learned about it one September Saturday when we were visiting one of my mother's many uncles. I wandered out to a crumbling tenant house being used as a grading shed, and listened outside for a moment. I heard nothing except the whisper of leaf on wood; the women inside were not talking.

I knocked and entered. Four black women of indeterminate age sat on wooden chairs with a grading frame in front of each, the frame little more than a wide horizontal plank with dowels set at intervals. Each cured leaf was examined and graded by these women for color and possible blemishes. When they had graded a small bundle, they would wrap the golden stems with another leaf, capping the ends with the wrapping leaf and add that hand to a neat, precisely swirled pile of its own grade.

A cured hand of high grade tobacco, capped and wrapped by someone who knows what she is doing, is a joy to the senses. The smell is so different from that of brandy, vanilla, and God-knows-what that tobacconists add, like the difference between the taste of real grapes and the taste of grape soda.

The broad golden leaf loses its vegetative feel during curing, becoming more like thin glove leather than leaf. Translucent when held up to the light, golden as honey or autumn sunshine, it feels warm as Baltic amber to the touch.

If the field hands were jokers and the barn crew gigglers, the older women graders were contemplative priestesses. Their deft hands were always moving with purpose and economy of motion, not hurrying to rush to judgment about a leaf. No blemish escaped them as they readied the golden harvest for the final judgment of auctioneers and buyers.

Their hands and the movement of the leaf had worn the grading frame so that it shone with patina on the wide, flat areas. The corners and edges were smooth as if milled. The women murmured when they spoke, which was seldom, the softness of their speech not even disturbing the dust imprisoned in the shaft of sunlight coming through the window.

Enterprising urchins in Greenville, Wilson, and Tarboro made a good profit picking up hands of tobacco that dropped from farmers' trucks and trailers on the way to the warehouses for sales. Those towns had an honest cured-tobacco smell, far different from Winston-Salem, which smelled of additives. Summers working in tobacco made me more money than a year of driving the school bus. After my junior year I had over a thousand dollars in my Zesta bank, even after buying my black clothes and shoes. I knew that I was going to college.

Miz Lewis seemed surprised when I turned up to take the SAT.

"You're going to college, Becca?"

"Yes, ma'm."

"Which one?"

"I haven't decided yet." I had, though.

Concentrating on doing my best, I looked up only once, to see Mr. Smythe watching me from the door. I was glad I was seated at a table by myself. He would have loved to claim I was cheating.

Weeks after the test as I walked through the hall to the library he called me into his office. I stood just inside the open door. "You know, Becca, you'll need a letter of recommendation from the school if you plan to get into college." His fat little face was wreathed in a "gotcha" smile.

"I won't if my scores are high enough." I didn't know if that was true or not, but I didn't care. I sauntered out of his office toward the library, where I sat shaking.

My scores were very high. I planned to enter college with the summer session that June. I drummed my mental fingers trying to make time pass. I could see the end. My plans were made and I knew I was going to make it. I gritted my teeth through the small town hoopla of the Senior Year. I would gladly have left sooner.

I used the time to ponder how I could get back at Mr. Smythe. The final PTA meeting in May was considered an important one for the parents. Mr. and Mrs. Smythe would have to be dead to have missed it. There was my opportunity.

The slope of Mr. Smythe's lawn was my challenge. All the children in town had longed to slide on that slope on the rare occasion when it snowed. With plastic trays or whatever we had commandeered as sleds we'd ring his doorbell to ask to slide.

"No, sir-ee Bob!" he would say. "I've busted my butt planting azaleas on that hill and I'm not going to have them stomped down." We'd promise to stay out of the azaleas, but he seemed to love depriving us from safe sliding fun.

Mr. Smythe kept his lawn fertilizer, which was white beside the spreader in his garden shed. After dark on the night of that last PTA meeting, I took a box of birthday cake candles and paced off the lawn, placing candles at the ends of the letters I had chosen. The lawn spreader had a little squeak in the wheels, but I worked rapidly, the little candles guiding me up the long slope. My letters were large, almost twenty five feet high and one lawn spreader wide. "FUCK YOU!," I wrote.

Dumping the remainder of the fertilizer at the side of the hill, I rolled the spreader down to the edge of the creek. It hissed as it sank into the dark water.

The message on Mr. Smythe's lawn was clearly visible from where I sat on graduation day, even though I had seen the fat little man mowing it that morning in a pants-whistling frenzy. I tried to keep the "gotcha" smile off my face.

I left the next day, so scared that even now I shake when I think about it. Early in the morning I took my clothes and the few other college things I had collected down to the Guinea Hole in my duffle bag, chaining it to the painter and around the tree before getting into the canoe. Never before was I so careful getting off on the hammock. Bob, the cottonmouth, was waiting for me on the mill stone. He eased himself insolently into the water when I splashed him with the blade of my paddle. Knowing there might be others, I whacked the mill timbers. There were no more. Bob ran a tight ship.

The clematis vine hiding my nail ladder was budding, with a few clusters already in bloom. As I reached the cavity in the tree, I almost fell, weak with relief at finding the Zesta can still there and still heavy. The 2,156 dollars, mostly in twenties, made quite a bundle in my purse.

After briefly considering letting the canoe drift to freedom down the creek, I snapped the lock on the painter and slung my duffle bag over my shoulder. I waited in the brush beside highway 64 until I heard the bus, then stepped out to wave it down. The driver helped me get my duffle inside.

"Visiting?" he asked.

"College," I replied.

8

Her jadedness was studied. From her lofty sophomore perch she descended into freshman naivete to guide me through the paperwork jungle of finding my assigned room and granting me a key. This princess of the tobacco belt had hair as dark as walnut wood with a startling four-inch wide streak of birch in the front. From my ornithology books the phrase "adventitious coloration" sprang into mind. She had obviously brushed up against something, causing the blonde to rub off on her.

I was the first student to arrive at Cotton Dorm that day. The bus had gotten me into Greenville at dusk the previous evening. Since I didn't have any place to go and didn't know a thing about getting a hotel room, I spent the night sitting on the commode in one of the pay toilets. I did know to safeguard my duffle with most of my money inside in a locker.

The night was jagged. I alternated dropping off to sleep and waking with a start. In mean, little sentence-long dreams, my locker key kept falling out of my bra and into the toilet, a knock on the stall door signaling my father. I could see his shoes under the door and knew it was him. Sometimes he would knock me and my locker key into the toilet bowl and activate the flush lever with his foot. Each of these anxious dream-sentences was myotonic, waking me with a jerk.

The sophomore snapped her Dentyne every time she clenched her teeth. Slapping a stack of cards and mimeographed sheets down on the desk in front of me, she said, "Fill 'em out. Ink."

The very first card was a locator card to be kept forever in the Dean of Women's office. It began

PARENTS' NAME: _____

PARENTS' ADDRESS: _____

_____

PARENTS' TELEPHONE: _____

Deception flowed from me so easily I almost smiled. Writing "Deceased" in a firm hand, I went on to the next questions. By the time I finished, I was feeling muzzy from lack of sleep and sustained excitement. The tobacco princess, brown as a berry, her two-toned hair smooth as a Breck girl's, drummed the fingers of one hand on the desk in syncopation with the activation of the retractor on her ball point pen and her gum. It must have taken me twice as long as a normal freshman to finish it all, I thought.

I passed the whole stack back for her perusal. "Parents dead?" I nodded, my eyes down. "Tough shit."

Was there no end to sophomore empathy? "Scholarship." The word almost didn't make it past the wallowing wad of gum.

"Huh?"

"Scholarship. Dead folks. You can git one. Lotsamoney."

She took out a little booklet and motioned me around the desk, clicking her pen. Circling the representation of a building on a map in the booklet, she proclaimed, "Scholarship office."

I was so tired. All I wanted was to stretch out on the cool tile floor, prop my head on my duffle, and sleep forever. She held up a bronze key. "Room 444. Five bucks deposit on the key. Cost you fifty cent to use the skeleton if you lock yourself out, OK?" I nodded and handed her five dollars.

My duffle got bigger and heavier with every flight of stairs. All the rooms on the floor stood open. Each was exactly like 444, with two twin beds made of blond wood, two matching dressers, two desks with little, built-in bookcases and two closets. In the corner over near the wall stood a sink flanked with two towel racks. Would I have a roommate? I tried my key in the lock and learned how to snap the little button on the inside to lock the door. Tossing my duffle onto the desk I sat on the bare mattress for a moment to savor the fact that the door was indeed locked.

I woke to the heat of the afternoon and the noise of doors slamming on the long hall. "You're gonna get cooties, layin' on that mattress tickin' like that."

I jumped. My roommate was sitting on the other bed across from me. "B. Linda Etherage. I go to Meredith. Gotta pick up some math this summer. Meredith don't have summer school." I introduced myself.

"Did you know we're across the courtyard from a couple of queers?" She went to the window and pointed across and down to the second floor on the other side.

"They're in the room with the blue curtains. You'd think they'd pull the shade or somethin'. They've been makin' out all afternoon. I heard this place was full of Lezzies." She looked at me sharply as if waiting for me to 'fess up.

The news that females could be queers was first on the what-I-learned-in-college list. I knew about male homosexuals, of course. I knew plenty of them: normal ones like Beau Lef' and strange ones like the Hardison boys who sang and played guitars in a gospel group, as dark and brooding as Beau Lef' was effusive and open.

Judge Sheppard Berkley seemed to qualify. He was an ancient, adenoidal man with audible post nasal drip. A retired judge, he lived with two old maid nieces who owned the movie theater in Plimpton. After retiring from the bench, he spent most of his time at the movies trying to trade candy for feels from the children in the theater. Shep Berkley preferred boys, and little ones at that, but he would also barter with little girls if they were closer. Puerile moviegoers learned quickly to listen to the soundtrack with one ear and keep the other for the approaching Judge.

He wasn't hard to keep track of, really. We'd listen for the shuffling of his little old man boots, the kind with elastic inserts on the sides, and the snuffling from his post nasal drip. When he got closer than one aisle away, like a flight of shorebirds seeming to be guided by a single brain, the whole bunch of us would rise and move to another part of the theater.

Shep Berkley always had pockets full of Raisinettes and Junior Mints and those big candy bars that were unavailable at the store. I always wondered whether his affliction was age or arthritis or all that candy. In my mind, Judge Berkley fell into the homosexual group.

I racked my brain to think of women I had known who could have been "Lezzies." The only ones who came to mind, who could even approach this newly formulated list were Sister and June Satterthwaite. I knew about Sister and June a decade and a half before I realized that their condition started with an "H" instead of an "M" (for "'morphodite"). They lived on a huge farm at the mouth of Mackey's Creek where the creek was protected and wide as a river, a favorite place for water skiing teenagers when the wind was up and the Sound too choppy. When the Sound was rolling, fishermen would also scoot into the protected creek to fish for perch and jacks. Poor folks with wire nets the size of a mattress scooped shoals of shad and herring for corning.

June and Sister's lawn swooped down from the big old house to the creek. The bank was firm, ending in a small pier. The best feature of the lawn, though, was the pump. There was always water to prime it, and even city children could get the friendly old pump to bring up tooth-numbing water, sweet as could be. Most cupped their hands under the flow and drank from their palms, but Sister and June left a small embossed jelly jar there for those who needed a cup. After a sun-drenched day on the Sound many a person stopped for a drink of water at "'Morphodite's Landing." Young and old would cut their eyes furtively to catch a glimpse of Sister and June. Some folks said they had seen the two; a few actually had.

Sister and June stayed to themselves, only going into town every month or so, always when children were in school.

Kay Dillon and I were in her father's Commodore the day we saw them. Kay and I had a relationship that intersected only in the summer, and then only because of water skiing. She loved to ski as much as I loved to drive the boat. The Commodore was twenty feet long and built of mahogany. An inch wider and we couldn't have launched at Mackey's Landing, saving us a fifteen mile drive to Owen's Landing on the Sound.

After a breezy day on the water, Kay and I were almost desiccated by the intensity of the sun. I steered the boat, Kay in tow, up into the creek and over to the little pier, tying up while Kay stowed her skis in the boat. The dappled light reflected by the dark water of the creek and the deep shade of the swampy vegetation began triggering the aura that would become a full-blown migraine unless I nipped it in the bud. Taking the aspirin tin from my purse I headed toward the pump.

Its handle was cool in the shade. I thought briefly about swallowing the tablets with the prime water, but decided against it. As I moved the handle I felt the uneven resistance of the leather diaphragm inside; it needed the prime water. Hurriedly I poured it into the throat of the pump, my hand over its mouth to trap any water rising or overflowing, while I pumped the handle. My vision was closing in fast. The aura, yellow and lime green neon hexagons, were flickering in the dark viscosity of my inner eye. Wrenching open the aspirin tin I shook three tablets into my palm, then reached for the jelly jar.

"Let me fill that for you, honey," came a man's voice next to me. Nausea was sweeping me. I turned to pass him the jelly jar and realized through my panic that I was standing beside a 'morphodite.'

"Thank you, ma'm," I said.

She was standing directly into the sun. Through my blurred vision and watery eyes I could see she wore a long skirt with an apron over it. Though it was hot as blazes, she had pants on under the skirt. Her shoes were heavy brogans, big as a man's. She also wore a man's work shirt with long sleeves. An old timey bonnet adorned her head, its sash tied in a big floppy bow under her full beard. I dropped my aspirins on the grass.

She picked them up. "Three?" she questioned.

"I'm getting a migraine," I told her.

"Sister has migraines, too. Just a minute, I'll call her." The person who must have been June called "Sister!" in her deep voice.

Another form dressed like June stood in the sun. June said, "Sister, this child is getting a migraine."

"June, moisten this cloth in that cold pump water. We'll stretch the girl out in the shade." Sister's voice was as deep as June's.

Putting her big hand under my elbow she led me into deep shade, had me lie on the grass and close my eyes. Big hands positioned a cold damp cloth over my eyes. The fingers of my right hand were gently moved to hold the cool, wet jelly jar. Another large hand smoothed my hair. Then I heard their big feet clump away.

The nausea receded. The neon hexagons became dimmer. I might have napped for a couple of minutes. "Becca! Quick, they're gone!" Kay had left the safety of the boat to come save me.

Raising myself to an elbow I squinted around for Sister and June in the sunlight, but they were indeed gone. "I need my sunglasses, Kay." She flew across the lawn to retrieve them from the boat.

I put them on as I walked back to the pump. The leather diaphragm was still swollen, still able to maintain a seal. Rinsing out the cloth I draped it over the pump handle to dry.

Sister and June were not in the shade along the edge of the lawn. I stared at the house for a minute. A curtain moved, then moved again. I waved both arms over my head. The curtain moved in response. Maybe Sister and June Satterthwaite were homosexual, I didn't know.

"So, whacha majoring in?" B. Linda asked. Majoring? What did that mean?

"I don't know," I replied.

"You got time," she said. "I wish someone had told me to wait to decide. Whatcha gonna register for tomorrow?"

The information the college had sent me had mentioned registration, but I didn't have the slightest idea what it meant. "What would you suggest?"

"Listen, if I was you, I'd do this. When you get inside Wright auditorium, you'll see all the majors listed on tagboard signs with folks sittin' under 'em. Go to the shortest line and tell whoever's there you want to major in that. Ask the person to be your advisor. You gonna take all the hard shit during the summer, right?" I nodded. "So then go and sign up for history or English or math. Get your advisor to sign off on your card and you're outta there."

That's exactly what I did. On the very next day I became a physical education major; physical education had the shortest line. Mrs. Stalls was my advisor. She signed off on my registration card showing I was registered for general math, U.S. History, and Psychology 103, all required courses. I paid six weeks' tuition with twenty dollar bills before heading back to room 444 of Cotton Dorm.

I was reading the campus map when B. Linda came back in. "Whadja get?" I handed her my class card. She whistled through her teeth. "Jesus. You're takin' a full load."

B. Linda thumped my little map. "Whereya goin?"

"To the bookstore. I need three books."

"Nononono," she said. "You buy books from the bookstore when you absolutely have to. You never buy 'em new unless you have ta. C'mon." She pulled me into the hall and pointed to little notices taped to some of the doors. "See? These people are sellin' used books. You shop around for the prices. You gotta get 'em quick off the doors, though. You don't wanna have to buy 'em from the bookstore." I picked up my history text that night, and B. Linda and I decided to split a math book since we were in the same class. The next morning I walked through a couple of dorms searching the postings on the doors until I found the psychology text I needed before heading to class.

The psychology professor considered himself a reasonable man. He assigned book reports, gave us three test dates, and required us to have at least a nodding acquaintance with the entire glossary. That was fine with me. I loved words; I would love the glossary. I flipped through the book to the back and started reading. There were many words and terms new to me, many names I didn't recognize. I looked forward to the challenge.

Since the summer sessions lasted only six weeks, each class met for two hours each day. While the president's office was air conditioned, the classrooms, dorm rooms, any place a student might lurk, were not. They simmered from middle March to late October. During the summer months the campus was a steaming, reeking hell. Over the drifts of cigarette butts and candy wrappers, wads of gum, and half-empty Pepsi cups that adorned each portico of every edifice buzzed swarms of yellow jackets. By the middle of June, the summer hatching of those winged stingers realized in some insect intelligence that no matter how much humans swung and swatted they were no threat to them singly or in swarm.

Maybe the sticky, thickened, mostly evaporated syrup from the cola cups or the leftover crumbs of chocolate, so full of paraffin they remained in a solid state even in the sun of eastern Carolina, gave them courage that their non-collegiate sisters did not have. Or perhaps it was the additives in the tobacco they nibbled. Whatever, the yellow jackets became insolent, landing on the bare, salt-rich skin of a sweating arm or neck to crawl around with waving antennae looking for just the right place to thrust a stinger. This was usually enough to send a person shrieking and swatting into the heat of a classroom.

Any professor in summer school with a shred of decency allowed a ten or fifteen minute break after the first hour of class. Students would scramble out of the room, headed for the water fountain or the soda shop to replenish the liquid sweated away during that first hour of class. Some would stand with cold cans of pop pressed to their temples while smoking in the dim halls.

When I got back to my desk before the second hour of psychology class that first day I turned vacantly to the glossary again. The word seemed as benign as any on the page until my vision activated it. The moment it entered my mind through my eyes it began to writhe like a disgusting worm, trailing the slime of its definition behind it. "Incest: cohabitation or copulation between two closely-related people. Father-daughter incest is the most common."

Closing the book I tried to remain upright in my desk. I didn't want to throw up, but my stomach heaved. Neon hexagons began to flash and squirm at the edge of my vision. I reached for my sunglasses and put them on. My fingers touched the aspirin tin in my purse, and though I was young and green and embarrassed at my every movement, I walked out of the class and into the hall to the water fountain. I swallowed the four pills left in the tin, leaning against the rough coolness of the plaster wall for support. When I had more control, I went back into the classroom and took my seat.

The enormity of finding a word for what had happened to me revealed itself slowly. I took my sunglasses off and looked slowly around the room. The definition was in the book. Its author had never asked me about it. It must mean that incest happened to someone else, maybe even to someone else in this room! "Who?" my mind breathed. Who else had fathers who raped them? Who else had their chests crushed by the weight of fathers, their vaginas ripped and torn? The other girls and women, in their Madras plaid shirts and skirts and their Weejuns without socks, sat expressionless, their faces telling me nothing about them. I searched their eyes for a sign that would let me know that they had experienced the violence of their fathers during dark nights, the terror of abuse during endless days. I saw not a glimmer of revelation, not a hint of shared experience.

"None of them know about this," my mind said. They are all the children of Ward Cleaver, and Ward never had intercourse with a child. He didn't even have a daughter. He only had Wally and The Beav. Was I was the only one in the class who had experienced incest? Perhaps, but somewhere there were others. Why else would there be this definition in this psychology book? I dropped my eyes from the faces of these simple, unknowing women and tried to think what to do, where to go for information.

Immediately after class I got out my campus map to locate the library, practically running across the wide green quadrangle to get to it. I didn't know libraries could be so big. This one was several floors high. The Plimpton library would have fit into one corner of the first floor. I saw a woman seated at a desk marked "Information" but immediately rejected the notion of asking where to find information about incest. She would have probably rent her garments, plucked out her eyes, and bolted for the phone to summon the campus police. Instead I asked how to get a library card.

My intuition was right about her. She was skittish, dedicated to keeping seekers of knowledge from the source of that which would set them free. She gave me a mimeographed sheet listing places in the library where I could not go, books not allowed to leave the library, and books not available to me at all. The experience was oddly reassuring. It took me back home to the Plimpton library. I could almost smell Miz Swain's fetid breath as she watched over my shoulder to keep me from looking up dirty words in the big Webster's. Once more I would have to find a way to get what I needed.

The woman pointed to the card catalog. It too was familiar, big oaken cases full of long drawers with cards. I went directly to the subject area. Finding the "I" drawer I pulled it, my fingers trembling. I found "incest" just after "Inca."

My nerve seemed to be oozing out of me, but I made myself look at the cards. There were only three references, each written before World War II. Making an effort toward legibility, I scribbled titles, authors and pertinent numbers on a sheet of notebook paper and stuffed it into my purse as I started back through an open door to where I could see the books.

"Badge number, please," said a voice out of the gloom just inside the door.

"Badge?"

"I need to see your badge. You're a grad student, right?"

"No."

"You work here? In the TV studio?"

"No."

"Then what the hell are you doing back here?"

"I've come to get a book."

A hand was on my arm, turning me to the light. "Shit. Freshman, right? You can't just sashay back into the stacks, girl. You gotta take your request to the main desk. They'll get your book for you." The voice stepped into the light. He wasn't much older than I. "You do have a library card, don't you?" His voice was filled with the sarcasm of one who controls a tiny crumb of the cosmos and who fully intends to lord that bit of power over the unsuspecting, the weak, or the naive.

I nodded. "Sorry," I added.

He retreated into the gloom. "Don't let it happen again."

At the main desk, I asked, "Could you please tell me how to get a book?"

The student behind the desk rolled her eyes as only a sophomore can. She asked in measured tones, "You do have a library card, don't you?" I nodded. "Then gimme the numbers and I'll get it for you," she sighed.

"I haven't decided what I want yet. Is there any way I could just see....."

"No way, hon. Grad students and people who work in the library are the only ones allowed in the stacks. Sorreeeee!"

I could see just how sorry she was. She slapped down another mimeographed sheet in front of me outlining in excrutiating detail the process for checking out a book.

"How do you get a job in the library?"

"Check the kiosk." She pointed at the big cylinder in the middle of the lobby.

Behind the convex glass of the kiosk hung notices and lists of part-time student jobs. I edged along around it, disappointed at the number of positions already scratched out, obviously taken. Halfway around was a posting on top of the others, as if just pinned onto the pile. It read:

> Audio Technician
> Campus TV
> Apply in person at studio upstairs

Audio technician? Campus TV? This was new to me, but it sounded like something I could do. Audio was sound, right? Perhaps the job had something to do with music. Besides, the TV studio was in the library, up on the top floor. It would be perfect for me. I needed a job anyway, and this could give me access to the books I wanted.

It took a moment for the woman at the information desk to acknowledge me. "I want to apply for the audio job with Campus TV," I told her.

"You're a freshman, right? They never hire freshmen up there. And they never hire girls."

"I do want to apply, though. Can you tell me where to go?"

She exhaled loudly. "OK, but you're wasting your time." She stood to point out the portico. "Go out those glass doors. See the ones on the left? Go up the stairs there to the fourth floor and you'll see signs to Campus Radio and TV. You're wasting your time, though."

At the top of the stairs I opened the door with a TV logo on it. A woman with long reddish hair pulled back into a smooth French twist sat behind the desk. "I'd like to apply for the audio job," I told her, more calmly than I felt.

She exhaled a stream of blue smoke. "You've had experience in audio?" "No, but I love music."

A little smile twitched on her lips. Had I said the wrong thing? "What kind of music?"

"I guess Baroque is my favorite right now. Handel," I added, in case she didn't know.

"Handel, huh?" She smiled that little smile again. "Are you a music major?"

"No, PE."

"PE!" She was incredulous. "You don't look like a PE major."

"They had the shortest line at registration. I just signed up for regular basic courses, though."

The woman stood up and stuck out her hand. "I'm Corinne Roush. The students call me Corinne or Doc. Sit down."

I sat and introduced myself. She asked about my work experience. I told her about the field work, about working in tobacco, about driving the school bus for two years. When she glanced at her watch the second time, I felt sure she wasn't going to give me the job.

"Becca, do you have class next period?" I didn't. "Put your stuff there," pointing at a line of lockers. Since my purse held the wad of twenties, I kept it with me as I followed her toward a big heavy door thick with double-glazed glass. Lights blinked as we went inside.

"Ross," Corinne said to a man with a clipboard, "This is Becca. She's our new audio person. I'll train her enough to get us through the next hour. You'll have to work around her schedule." In fifteen seconds she showed me what to do for the next hour. "See this dial? It's called a pot. Your job right now is to work the pot so that this needle," she pointed to it, "stays between here and here."

"That's it?"

"For the next hour, that's it. Ross'll show you how to check out the equipment, mikes and all."

She motioned to Ross. "She's a country girl, Ross. She's used to getting up at the crack of dawn. This is the person you've been looking for."

Ross had obviously been hoping for more than an early riser. "5:30?" he asked. Struck dumb, I nodded.

"OK," he shrugged. "Doc, get her a badge."

My heart was thumping. I had a job. I had a badge. The library was mine, a bloodless coup! If I'd had a minute to think about it, I might have been tempted to run. Compared to really professional studios, ours was small potatoes, but all I could see was complexity: banks of dials, monitors stacked on top of monitors, and two mobile cameras, both black and white. Color TV was mainly a rumor for most of us, although a few had actually seen it.

I sat in the audio technician's chair and put my hand on the pot. Nothing happened. Ross said, "Put on the earphones."

Though the earphones were cumbersome compared with modern ones, their heaviness was comforting, substantial. Even the slight pinch over my ear felt comforting, lending reality to the situation.

In three hours that day I learned what the various switches were for, savoring being on such a cutting edge of technology, repeating in the mouth of my mind the jargon of the studio. "Cut. Punch up. Fade. Zoom. Dolly in." I loved it.

Corinne gave me a temporary badge on the way out. "You'll

have to have a photo ID. Maybe tomorrow you can get it, but this'll get you past the guard in the morning. How did you get up here today?" I hesitated. "Did you come up the stairs or use the elevator?"

"The stairs."

She came around the desk and said, "Use the elevator. I'll show you." The elevator was down the hall just past the doors to the studio. "In the morning look for a button on the stanchion beside the main door outside. Ring it and the guard'll come and let you in. The doors you went through today are locked in the morning." She led me into the elevator, and I examined the unfamiliar buttons until it came to a lurching stop. Walking through stacks we arrived back at the lobby. I could hardly believe my luck. I wanted to ask about the other floors, but decided not to tip my hand, to show interest that might seem undue. I would check the other floors myself. I would find the books about incest. My badge and my reason for being in the library was assured.

Back at room 444, B. Linda was unpacking the tangle of boxes and tossing clothing into piles on her bed. "I have two bedspreads. Hope you don't mind." She nodded toward my bed. A red, whipcord bedspread covered my sheets.

"Oh, thanks." I hadn't even thought of needing a bedspread. Her bedspread, a match to the one on my bed, lay crumpled under a pile of panties, bras and half slips. The matching curtain billowed in the breeze from the window.

"Your stuff coming later?"

"Nope."

"You got it stored?"

"Nope. This is it."

Her eyes swept my side of the room. "Shit," she said. "All you got is an alarm clock?" I pointed to my Motorola.

"Shit," she said again.

Flipping down the bedspread and the sheet, I put my desk chair on the bed, fixing it with a pillow into a back rest for reading, as I had seen girls do sunning in the courtyard.

"Thought maybe we could study math together," I invited.

"OK," said B. Linda distractedly. Then, with her hand on her hip and tapping her foot, she asked, "You gonna use all your drawers?" It was obvious she had looked through my stuff.

"Just the top one. Feel free."

She started dumping her tangled belongings into the drawers on my side. "This is really all ya got? You poor or somethin'?"

I thought of the two thousand dollars in my purse. "Not really. I travel light."

"Daphne said you're an orphan."

"Daphne?"

"She works down at the desk. She said that you're on scholarship." Her eyes hovered on my alarm clock again. "I guess they don't give you much when you leave the orphanage."

This was getting out of hand. I'd have to scotch it. "I live with my grandmother, B. Linda. Daphne must have assumed that I lived in an orphanage. I don't have a scholarship. I plan to work my way through college."

Her eyes were big. "Waiting tables? For four years?"

"I have a job in television." It slid from my lips.

"Television? You mean TV? What channel? What time are you on?"

"I'm an audio technician. I'm not on."

"Oh." She was disappointed. "Well, maybe they'll let ya be on after a while." She stuffed some more clothing into my chest of drawers.

"Anyway," she added, as if an afterthought. "I thought you might be a nigra."

I almost dropped the math book. "What?"

She was defensive. "They're gonna let 'em in the state schools, you know. It's just a matter of time before Earl Warren stuffs 'em down all our throats. I was afraid you'd be a nigra or a lezzie." She looked at me sharply again.

"Relax, B. Linda. I'm a white orphan who works in television."

The television part seemed to cheer her again. "Could you believe that math class? I was sitting so far back I could hardly see that old man. There's more in that class than in the whole freshman class at Meredith." She pulled open another drawer. "Becca. What kind of name is that? I was scared it might be a ni..." She froze, knowing she was on the cusp of disaster. "Is it short for somethin'? Rebecca or somethin'?"

It became clear that B. Linda said everything that passed through her mind. She did not consider or reconsider anything. If she thought it, she said it. It was sure to be a limitation for her in the future.

"B. Linda, my name is Becca. It's not short for anything. Do you want to study math?"

"Nah. You don't have to study in Doc Weaver's class. Why do you think there's 437 people in that auditorium? Everybody in the world knows he passes the whole class."

She sat down on my bed and took the math book out of my hand. "Listen. This is how it works. Old Weaver gives those who over-cut a D. If you cut four times you get a C, three times and you get a B. Get it? All you gotta do is show up!" She tossed the book onto the desk as if it offended her. "My case is different, though. Everything I take transfers back to Meredith as a C anyway. I'll sleep in some mornings, probably when I have my period. I feel like shit then."

I slid past her to retrieve my book. She might be right, but I still planned to study.

In the morning I found the buzzer just where Corinne said I would and rode the elevator up to the studio. Ross nursed a cup of coffee as if it were life-giving. He mumbled orders and I complied. Finally at seven thirty when the rest of the crew straggled in, wiping sleep crystals out of their eyes, he said to me, "Good," and pointed to my chair beside the technical director.

Our eight o'clock show was Psychology 103, the same class I was taking, but taught by Dr. Pritchett, the head of the department. So many students needed the class as part of their core curriculum that the college televised it, as well as other classes. Students by the hundreds packed into auditoriums to watch huge TV monitors. Graduate students acting as monitors checked the class rolls but didn't require ID. There was a brisk business of people who, for a fee, would fill the seats of absent students.

The tests were standardized, "for fairness to all students" trumpeted the catalog, but we all knew it was merely expedient. Copies of tests were best-sellers and gradually answer sheets were too, as those who could afford them grew bolder and lazier. The sheer numbers of students, the crush, seemed to overwhelm the support system. The academicians prattling about educational quality and ideals of student-staff ratio were brushed aside by accountants and registrars with stars in their eyes. We were ambergris on the shores of their financial woes. They would glean us, stack us like cordwood, process us. They could build more dorms, more classrooms, expanded libraries, bigger stadia. Though classes and dorms grew more crowded, and only the rare student ever got to talk to a professor, tuition rose inexorably.

The system perpetuated itself. Its own inertia kept it moving, like smaller systems I had seen before. It rolled along because it was rolling along. Nothing was big enough to stop it. It gathered up all us students as in a lint brush, matted us together like a piece of felt, giving us all the same shoddy treatment. We were the masses. We got a Pizza Hut education.

A popular professor, someone with charisma, someone loved by students, was usually chosen to teach the TV courses. Dr. Pritchett was one of those. He was adored by his staff. The eyes of psychology majors would moisten at mention of his name. He was an excellent teacher and a nice man besides.

When the little red light over camera two flashed on, that nice man, that excellent teacher, froze. He glanced repeatedly from the corners of his eyes as if expecting disaster to arrive from just out of camera range. Speech seemed almost impossible to him because of lack of breath. He spoke in clauses and phrases, his mind apparently wandering. His infrequent movements were as jerky as a puppet's. By the end of a show he was sodden from perspiration. Poor Dr. Pritchett needed an audience.

He would get nothing from the floor crew. Though they were also students, a year older than I, they had already over-identified with technicians everywhere, separate from and superior to on-air people. Smug in their knowledge of the studio's gadgetry, they made no effort to demystify the process for the academics who were pressed into roles as performers. The arrogance they felt in the ability to disconnect a person who had worked 15 years on his education and 15 more on his reputation was barely sheathed. Though they pretended not to notice Dr. Pritchett, they loved watching him flounder.

During my first week at the studio, as soon as I got over my shyness, I mentioned to Dr. Pritchett that I had enjoyed the movie about monkey mothers he had showed in class. "You listen!" He was incredulous.

"Sure."

Wise to the ways of technicians, he asked, "Why?"

"For a bunch of reasons. I'm taking Psychology 103 myself. You've cut my study time 75%. You're the head of the department. You're the best."

"What else? I never see you on the floor. Nobody else here listens." Did I hear petulance? Did this Lord of Learning, this Zeus of Psychology, this Academic Noble feel the slings and arrows of lowly, piss-ant technicians?

"Ok, Ok. I'm the audio technician. I monitor your sound to see that it goes out right. But I really do listen to you and enjoy it. There's a toggle switch I could use to control the pot without listening, but I enjoy your lectures."

"Show me where you work, darlin'." Back in the control room, he sat in my chair and put on the head phones. "I don't hear a thing." I flipped a switch so he could hear the chatter in the studio. He had me sit in the chair while he went outside and shaded his eyes trying to see me. "I can't see you, darlin'," he said plaintively. I turned on the little lamp that allowed me to cue the tape for the music appreciation class. "Better," he said. Turning the lamp toward my face I waved at him. "Perfect!" he chirped

Though my relationship with Dr. Pritchett grew and became cordial, it never occurred to me to ask him about books on incest. Instead, taking the sheet on which I had written the call numbers of three books, I skulked through the stacks at night and found them, one by one. I approached each volume feeling unreal, light as air, as though dreaming the whole thing. The trepidation I felt, the dread, seemed magnified by the surroundings of mustiness and gloom. Any thought of reshelving the old volumes, any idea of leaving the dimly lit area smelling of mold, old paper and museum pests never even crossed my mind. Sitting on the round wheeled library stepstools I read, listening for the elevator, for the footsteps of staff.

On consecutive nights for almost a week I read case studies of retarded girls in middle-European villages, made pregnant by their peasant drunkard fathers. I read of tropical cultures where the virginity of girls was a gift to the tribe, her father included, and of lust-ridden mothers who seduced ever-willing sons. Nowhere in these books did the half-witted, peasant daughters wear Madras shirts and go to college. Nothing was written about their lives after the incest, no documentation of later adventure or happiness, no mention of any hope, any recovery. There was no delineation or plan to help them with living.

The revelation from the readings was a pike through my heart. I could sit with the Madras shirts, even buy one to wear myself, but I could never be one of them. The disappointment at knowing the depth of my difference cut at my breathing, crushed my chest. I felt constricted, pulverized. I felt as though I were an iceberg calved from a glacier of shame and abnormality. Everyone else in my classes and those at work seemed to be little pleasure boats motoring from buoy to buoy following well-marked channels, while I drifted in waters uncharted and dark.

The only razor blades at the student store were the double-edged kind. At Kresge's, an old worn uptown store with wooden floors I found Blue Diamonds. "Scraping paint?" the woman at the cash register asked.

"Huh?"

"Just askin' if you're gonna use these for scrapin' paint off your windows. We sell a lot of 'em for that."

"Yeah."

Having the Blue Diamonds again was a comfort, making things seem more manageable in the knowledge they were in my dresser drawer. They were my Balm of Gilead, my check valve.

I would not have to endure the unendurable.

Though I could lock my door for the first time in my life, my nights were invaded by dreams in which I was immobilized. Two of them were repeated with such frequency I thought I was going insane. In one, there is a family gathering on an unscreened porch. An old woman sits in a porch swing at the end of the porch, while several other people who I knew in dreamlike certainty to be members of the family sit in old-fashioned metal porch chairs. A man in his early twenties is holding a very young baby dressed in a little cap with flowing ribbons and a christening gown. He is holding the child horizontally, leaning over her. In the dream I am able to see the fear in the eyes of the baby. I know the child is me.

In the second dream I watch myself standing at a bus stop. The landscape is barren, with no grass or trees or shrubbery. As a man approaches my clothing becomes transparent and stands away from my body as if held by the ribs of an umbrella. The man comes nearer and begins touching my body with spatulate fingers, leaving trails of mucous wherever he touches. I watch myself standing there with my head down, not moving, waiting for him to leave. The dream mutated slightly in later versions. I still wore transparent clothes and his fingers were still spatulate and trailing mucous, but in later dreams he wore a raincoat.

"You groan at night, Becca. You moan and grit your teeth. This is gettin' old, hon." B. Linda talked to Daphne at the desk and found herself another roommate. Instead of moving her things out of the dressers, she and her new roommate merely switched chests of drawers from one room to the other.

The green and yellow neon hexagons flickered in my vision with regularity. Though my head pounded with migraines, I kept up my classwork.

"Becca, are you working too many hours?" Corinne asked one day. I felt dulled out by pain and vomiting. Had she found out that I plundered the stacks at night? Had she followed some paper trail to the books on incest? "Do you need to cut back on hours, Becca?"

If she cut my hours I'd have to get a job in a restaurant. "No."

I said.

"Becca, are you pregnant?"

"God, no! What makes you think that?"

"You have circles under your eyes and you've been throwing up in the bathroom for the past two weeks."

Groaning, I confessed, "I have migraines, Corinne."

"Who has migraines?" Dr. Prichett was standing at the office door.

"Becca does."

He came over to my chair and patted my shoulder. "Darlin'," he said, his voice full of sympathy. "Jesus Christ, I used to have 'em so bad..." He picked up the telephone on Corinne's desk and dialed. "Irena Steele, please. This is Sam Pritchett."

"Good," said Corinne.

"Irena, this is Sam. One of our best workers over here at the studio has just been laid low by migraines. Could you please see the child?" He waited with his hand over the mouthpiece. "Can you go to the infirmary at 4, darlin'?" he asked me. I nodded.

9

"You're not pregnant, are you?"

The needle was very thin. I hardly felt it prick my skin. "No."

"This'll make you sleep, Becca. I'll make rounds tonight and check on you." Irena Steele put her cool hand on my forehead again. I felt myself sliding into sleep.

I didn't know what time it was when she returned. I had just awakened and was trying to decide whether or not I could find the bathroom. She tapped gently on the door and entered, closing it quickly, knowing how the light made my head pound. "Feeling any better?"

"Yeah." I sat up and swung my legs over the side of the bed.

"Where do you think you're going?"

"I'm feeling better. I've gotta get back to the dorm."

"I took the liberty of signing you out, Becca. I told them you'd sleep here at the infirmary. You were sleeping so soundly, and I wanted to observe you for a time."

I eased my weight onto my feet. "Bathroom," I muttered.

Sitting on the toilet in a swirl of white tile and chrome, I tried to think what had happened while I was asleep. How had she known which dorm I lived in? What had she told anyone there? The early 60's were a repressive time for college girls at the mercy of tenacious administrators. Though my head still pounded, the nausea had receded. I had to get back to the dorm and cover the lies I had told.

Dr. Steele was waiting in my room. I sat on the edge of the bed and slipped my shoes on. "I really do have to get back. I get up early. Work starts at 5:30, warming up the equipment and..."

"Becca, it's after midnight. The dorm has been closed for an hour and a half. Tomorrow is Saturday. You don't have to work." She had prepared another shot, waiting on a tray beside my bed. I sat back down on the bed.

"How long have your parents been dead?" It made me wince and she saw it. Taking my shoes off she helped me stretch out. "Since I was very young." I closed my eyes, putting my arm over them to block the light bleeding through my lids.

Her hands were on my arm, then I felt the needle slide into my flesh. "I'm going to put a note on your chart for you to stay until I check you out tomorrow, Becca." The medicine was moving through my body so fast I could hardly think of what to say.

The sun was coming through the area around the venetian blinds when I woke up. There was no clock, but I guessed it was after 8. When I returned from the bathroom, Dr. Steele was there.

"How are you feeling?"

"A thousand times better." I tried to exaggerate my relief to let her know I was ready to leave.

"How often do you have these headaches, Becca?"

"Oh, once a month," I lied.

"Around the time of your period?"

Was she going to examine me? She'd find out that... "That doesn't have anything to do with it." I felt panicky.

"You aren't taking those new birth control pills, are you, Becca?"

I laughed. It made my head ache a little and I put up my hand to try to press it away. "No need to. I don't date."

She smiled. "Too busy working, huh?"

I tried to head that off. "I enjoy it, Dr. Steele. I'm meeting some fantastic people. I'm learning a lot about an industry most people wonder at and I'm making my own way."

"Sure."

I could see she was not convinced. "I really enjoy what I'm

doing," I said as earnestly as I could. "The headaches? I've had 'em since I was eight, off and on. They come and go."

She reached over and took my hand. Surprised, she turned it palm up and traced the callouses left from spring work with the hoe. "My God."

I grinned girlishly. "This is easy work, Dr. Steele, and the pay is great."

She replaced my hand and sighed. "Becca, when you get these headaches, come over here. We'll help you with them. If you ever want to talk, just call me."

A prickling sensation came over me. Through the wooziness I thought briefly about telling her, now that I knew the word for it. But I couldn't look at her, so I busied myself with putting on my shoes. "Thanks." I knew I wouldn't.

I aced Psychology 103 that first semester without even studying. My A in history was earned, but not as hard as I had thought. The B in Math meant nothing; two hundred people in the class made at least that. Everyone passed, even B. Linda.

I didn't have a roommate second session, which was fine with me. I was busy, pulling the early morning shift at the station, taking a full load of courses, and reading in the stacks whenever I could. I didn't hang around the lounge of the studio like some of the others.

I was struck dumb around Corinne. She was a goddess to me. I overheard her telling someone about her schooling in England, how she had done brass rubbings to make tuition payments. Her car was a red Austin Healey with the steering wheel on the right. I stared when I saw her with it in the parking lot, stunned at being so near the ultimate of sophistication. Seeing my admiration, she grinned and motioned me over. "Get in, Becca. We've got time before next hour. I need some cigarettes." She pointed at the seat belts. "Buckle up!" I had never seen a seat belt. It was a struggle for me.

She eased the little car out of the parking space, then popped my head back as she sped out of the parking lot. I was breathless but beaming by the time we returned.

We walked inside toward the elevator. "How's the work coming? I see you studying back in the stacks sometimes."

I made myself keep walking. "Fine. I'm keeping up with everything."

"Good! By the way, David and I are having a party on Saturday. He's bringing people from the Music Department. I'm inviting English and all the TV teachers. I always ask the studio staff too, Becca. I'd love it if you could come."

It was just like in the books. Easy. Cultured. I was in a dream in which I knew just what to do. "I'd love to go, Corinne." It was as natural as the bounce of a ball, an echo, the beat of a heart.

She gave me a little hug. "Great. Now I know Sam Pritchett will be there. He'll have an audience." My God, these adults seemed to know everything. I had expected they would be smarter than the people I had known before, but there was something else about them. They received information with more than just their five senses, or perhaps they had a way of combining their reception, multiplying it somehow. They just seemed to know certain things as if with some core that I was unfamiliar with in other adults. I would have to sharpen my skills, to be more careful around them. Still, it was great to be invited. I managed a chuckle.

The fact that I had nothing appropriate to wear to the party nibbled on my conscious mind all day, becoming painfully clear when I perused my sparse wardrobe that evening.

I went looking for B. Linda, the only person I knew on campus, hoping she'd have something I could borrow. Daphne, still running the desk downstairs, still snapping her Dentine, told me that B. Linda had gotten her C in math and left after first session.

After classes and work the next afternoon I went downtown ready to spend some of the money from the Zesta can on a dress. I looked everywhere — Belks, Brodys, the Snooty Fox — but couldn't find the dress I wanted. In a panic, I walked through a fabric shop looking at the plaids and chintzes. They even had a bolt or two of Madras cotton, which surprised me. Nothing I saw would do.

On the way out, just inside the door, a piece of upholstery material on the remnant table caught my eye, a muted creamy beige with a thin stripe of smoky blue and slightly glossy flowers every inch or two. If I could match the blue and put piping around the neckline and arms, and cover a big button with the same blue fabric for the front of the dress, it would be perfect. I felt the fabric, expecting it to be heavy and stiff, but it was almost as light as dress fabric, surely more than adequate for the evening. I found a simple pattern, delighted that the boring days I had spent sewing in Mrs. Wilson's Home Ec classes would pay off within the week.

The Singer store displayed complex machines in wooden cabinets to look like fine furniture, costing hundreds of dollars past anything I could afford. The portable models were not much better and were very heavy besides. The look of the salesmen told me that renting a machine would also be out of the question. The "Used Machines" sign caught my eye. Most were table models, many of them looking quite new. A salesman answered my unasked question. "Repos," he said. "People can't make the payments. Give ya a good price on this here baby." He rubbed his hand across the top of a machine housed in maple-colored wood.

"No. Just looking." I spotted the portables on a long table along the side of the room.

Sensing my interest, he practically raced me over to the table and took the plastic cover from one little machine.

"Top of the line," he assured me. "Zigzag."

I spotted a wooden cover, indicating an old machine. Sure enough, it was black with gold Old English lettering, unlike the battleship gray and ivory green of the newer models. "Singer" it said. I couldn't help smiling at it. "Does it work?"

"Yeah, it works, but it ain't a zigzag. You ain't gonna make buttonholes with that old piece of junk."

"Where are the attachments?" I wondered if it had a zipper foot. I had to put in a zipper.

Disgusted, he pointed to the mechanism that allowed the machine to be lifted from the case. "Plug it in. 15 bucks if you want it." He went back into the showroom. In the tray under the machine I found a cardboard box of attachments, an instruction book, two tiny screwdrivers and a little wire-handled brush. There were at least fifteen bobbins and cotton thread on wooden spools. I sewed a few inches on a scrap of fabric and found it in perfect running order. I had decided to buy it when the salesman reappeared. "Take it for ten bucks," he said.

"No, I'll pay you fifteen, but you have to haul both of us over to Cotton Dorm."

He shrugged. "OK."

"Portable" is a relative term. I was exhausted by the time I got the machine to the third floor and set it up on the desk that would have been B. Linda's. I knew I could sew the dress and I loved owning the sewing machine.

The dress was ready two days before the party. I had managed a little tan on my arms and legs by studying in the sun court and could hardly stand waiting. This would be my first adult party.

The taxi driver found the house easily, though it was outside the city. Corinne answered the doorbell. "Becca! I'm so glad you came." Her expression changed abruptly and I knew that something was wrong. Had she forgotten she had invited me? Had I done something to offend her? She blocked my way, then took me aside on the front porch. "Becca, there is something you should know." What had I done? What had happened? Would I die right there on the porch? She gave me a quick hug and kissed me on the cheek. "Take a deep breath, Becca. You've gotta know this before you go inside."

"What?" I felt faint.

"Becca, I've got a chair just like your dress."

For one second I was stunned, then relief and laughter bubbled right out of me. Corinne and I leaned against each other and bellowed with laughter.

She wiped her eyes. "Listen, we can move the chair. You can come in through the kitchen and I'll throw a cloth over the chair. No one will know." She was wiping her eyes, laughing again.

"Nope. No." I shook my head, screwed up my courage and walked inside. Some of the people in the living room had heard us laughing outside. A stunned silence accompanied my walk across the living room floor. In the middle of the oriental rug in front of the chair I did a twirl, sat down in the chair and put my feet up on the matching ottoman. Laughter roared from the people in the room. Those in the dining room came in to see what was so funny, their laughter echoing as they realized what had happened.

Sam Pritchett, who had seen the whole thing, hustled over. He sat on my lap and kissed me on the cheek. "I knew you were a honey, but I didn't know you were a suite!" he hooted. Like most psychologists, Dr. Pritchett believed that punning was a sign of intelligence. He never missed a chance. People shrieked again. Everyone loved Sam Pritchett.

For a moment I remembered my grandmother making Beau Lef' and the trustees laugh. She would have loved this.

Dr. Pritchett moved from my lap to the ottoman, where he sat for the rest of the evening, not letting me get up for anything. He brought me my first drink and a plate of hors d'oeuvres. Before long we were in the center of a knot of his friends and admirers. Sam Pritchett was the kind of person who made people shine, as I did that night. Because of him and because I sat in the chair, I met everybody at the party, faculty and students, and gained a tiny reputation as a witty person. It was a wonderful, heady experience, helping me understand the look of conquest on Grandmother's face when she made people laugh.

Corinne drove me back to the dorm in the Austin Healey. She put the top down and we laughed all the way. Daphne looked up as I signed in. "Great dress," she said.

I couldn't help giggling. "Drunk?" she asked.

"In a manner of speaking."

Between shows on Monday Corinne asked me to house-sit for her between the last session of summer school and Fall quarter. She and Dave would provide food and pay me twenty dollars a week. The Healey was off limits, but Dave would let me drive his VW in return for taking them to the airport in Raleigh and picking them up. All I'd have to do was feed their cat and leave bacon out for the mouse that nested in their paperback books in the den.

I was almost too stunned to reply. I hadn't given any thought to the school break or where I would be. How perfect could it be? The run of their house, a car, and no expenses. I nodded.

"What do you want from Paris?" she asked.

Paris! My heart turned over in my chest. "Perfume," I told her.

"Joy." She laughed.

Those seventeen days were the closest I had ever come to a real vacation. Almost every day I went to the beach, the little family beach on the nearby Pamlico River when driving didn't appeal. On other days the ocean called. Picking a book from the bookcase that covered the entire wall, I would pack a sandwich and drive to Morehead City. When the sun got too hot or the biting, greenhead flies too obnoxious I would swim in the clear waves. It was a wonderful, relaxing time.

Corinne told her friends about my good job house-sitting, and there was never a holiday that I didn't have a job and a new place to enjoy.

She also recommended me to the commercial TV station managers in town. I filled in during the vacations of the technical crew and on weekends, witnessing there the same snobbery as in the ranks of the technicians at our little campus station.

Some on-air personalities collected scorn and ridicule as if they had flypaper for skin. Sherwin Hofstatler, the weatherman who doubled as Billy on the Cactus Billy Show, was one. No one knew why Sherwin had chosen television as a career. The black and white of the medium at that time suited him perfectly; Sherwin was gray. He read the weather information into the camera in a monotone.

Once he tried using a pointer as a prop, but instead of using it to point to a specific weather-stricken area, he held it in one place as if indicating the map as a whole. For almost a month he delivered weather news that way, standing, reading, with the pointer in his left hand, never moving. Some staffer (or as we liked to fantasize, an irate viewer) put an end to the use of the pointer. Sherwin went to the umbrella stand where he kept it and found it capped with a latex birth control device, viscous fluid dribbling from it.

The poor man was no better on the Cactus Billy Show. His set was pathetic: a bale of hay, a cardboard saguaro cactus and a wooden fence that fell down at least once during every show.

Children, card-carrying members of the Cactus Billy Club from Bear Grass, Whitley, Jamestown and Goldhill, came in their parents' station wagons to sit behind the flimsy wooden fence on the little bleachers to watch obscure, flickering old cowboy movies. Even the children were obviously unimpressed by Cactus Billy. They found the movies deadening. Some of them slept on the show. One little buckeroo fell off the bleachers and knocked down the fence. Their parents wanted them to be on television. They dressed the kids up in their best clothing and took them to the station after school. The children were always white, and always subdued.

Sherwin's Cactus Billy costume was as drab as he, with fuzzy chaps, an embroidered vest, and a cowboy hat two sizes too small. Worst of all were his gun and holster, so obviously plastic that even the kids rolled their eyes. He was as disgusting a cowboy as he was a weatherman.

Sherwin's duties as a weatherman were simple: remove copy from the Ampex and read it on the air. Though his job did not include analyzing weather data or extrapolation of ideas from facts, he began to take his weatherman's position seriously. He answered an ad for a home weather forecasting kit. We pointed out to him that it was a plastic child's toy, but he was undaunted. He set the instruments up in the median strip between the two parking lots, and every night when the crew shut down the station the men would urinate in Sherwin's rain gauge. He never caught on.

As numbing as the Cactus Billy Club and Sherwin's weather forecasting were, Sundays were stultifying, once small town live TV was introduced into the Bible Belt. With the proliferation of Blue laws, people had no reason to leave their homes before noon except to go to church. From nine to eleven we broadcast two church programs.

Though different in presentation, the two were much alike, as far as I could see, in product. At nine o'clock, The Reverend Doctor I. Marion Wheaton spoke for one hour about the hell that awaited us, in tones chilling for lack of affect, and deadening in its sameness Sunday after Sunday.

At ten minutes to ten Brother Ithamus Harrison would blow like a whirlwind into the lobby. Most of the time, if we were lucky, he'd have singers with him, dressed in satin robes. Many times I wished we could have broadcast in color.

If the Reverend Doctor Wheaton's message was sheathed in cold steel, Brother Harrison's was as warm as the inside of your mouth and as saucy as a cinnamon stick.

During the hour-long broadcast of Doctor Wheaton's message, we changed cameramen at least twice to avoid the repetition of the service when a cameramen had locked in on the good doctor, hooked an arm over the camera and fallen asleep. No one in the control room had seen it; we were all either dozing or sound asleep.

One Sunday morning as I fought to stay awake I noticed the director, Dean, another student, playing around with a funeral home calendar, focusing on it with camera two. In our fight with Sunday ennui, we had all played around with the Reverend Doctor Wheaton's image, making his face long and thin, or making the picture shimmy and roll just enough to get those lie-about Christians off their duffs and over to the TV to fix it.

Then very faintly on the monitor I saw the image of Jesus praying at Gethsemane. Dean allowed it to stay there just a moment before making it disappear. Two minutes later the switchboard began to buzz. The church-viewing public had witnessed a miracle. They had seen Jesus in their TV set. Dean and the rest of us on duty that Sunday were ready to plead for our jobs.

When the Reverend Doctor Wheaton heard of the interest generated by the superimposed picture from the calendar, he smiled for the first time in memory. He looked over the other pictures in the calendar to choose shots of Jesus on The Cross and The Angel Sitting on The Rock for the following Sunday. The superimposition of religious pictures became de rigueur for Dr. Wheaton.

When Brother Ithamus Harrison was informed of the wispy images of Jesus appearing like a miracle behind Dr. Wheaton, he informed us that as a member of the NAACP he did not have to put up with such shoddy treatment and would take his business to another station if those pictures weren't hanging in the air behind him on the very next show. We were delighted to oblige.

I socialized a little with the crew after work but never dated any of the men. The men — boys, really — I dated were carefully picked. I was sure they expected nothing of me sexually.

Rafael Medina was from Spain, a lieutenant in the US Air Force. Every Wednesday he called me from the base, speaking quietly in lovely English with a lisping Spanish accent, asking me to dinner the next weekend. After dating him for months, I hardly ever remembered him from one week to the next. When he asked me to marry him it first occurred to me that I would never marry. I returned the huge emerald and diamond ring he offered me. I never saw him again and seldom even thought about him.

Just after Fall quarter, before it got too cold to swim in the ocean, the crew from the college station went down to Atlantic Beach, just out of Morehead City. We took food and beer, planning to spend the weekend sleeping on the beach.

The weather was so lovely and the water so perfect for swimming we decided to cut Monday classes and go back on Tuesday, a seemingly simple decision that started a chain of events which gradually changed my life and helped me to begin dealing constructively with the incest and what it had done to me.

When I walked into my room at college, I found the Dean of Women, Dr. Brown, sitting on my bed. She had let herself in with a master key, and the wait had not sweetened her normally sour disposition. I stood there sweaty and gritty, burned to a crisp. I couldn't think of a thing to say. The look on her face said it all. I was in huge trouble. "You are a wicked, very disturbed girl," she began. What was she talking about? What could she have known? Had she found my Blue Diamonds? If it was just staying out overnight, I'd get detention, and that would be all right. I waited. She would tell me. They always did.

"When you weren't in your room Sunday night we assumed that you had slept over with a girl friend. You've never been caught for staying out before. When you didn't return by noon on Monday, we began checking, Becca." She said my name as if she knew me. I knew how to last through anything, though. I had learned well. I didn't raise my eyes to challenge her or give her the loathe-look. I stood as impassive as a statue.

She continued, "It might surprise you to know that your parents are not dead. It certainly surprised all of us here." She waited for a reaction. "Your parents are indeed living. You have lied to us here, Becca." She chewed her lips, then puffed a lungful of air through them.

I could see that the lying part was more important to her than the viability of parents. I thought briefly that the "us" might be the editorial "us," with no one else involved. The moment that thought hit my brain, every single cell knew it was grasping at straws. I knew better than to ask.

"When I talked to your parents on the phone..." The surf started roaring in my ears. It took all my strength to remain upright, to keep from vomiting. "...they agreed to sign a statement that they know you are here. They have been so cut, so hurt by your actions and the report of your absence that they agree that you should have help. We agree that if you are to stay here at college, you will have to be in counseling and never ever see that boy again."

What in the world? What had they told her? What boy? Rafe? I hadn't seen him this whole year and in any event they never knew about him, certainly not from me. They must have told her that I had been going home all those weekends, and made up some story about a local boy. They lied, pretending I was out with a boy. Suddenly authority had been inserted into their lives. I wondered if police were involved.

Whatever had happened, they had been frightened enough to lie. My mind raced to see how I could salvage this thing and not lose the ground I had gained.

Dean Brown's voice interrupted my thoughts. "If you stay at this institution, you will be on probation for the next six months. You will attend every therapy appointment..."

"I don't have the money for therapy, Dean Brown. I hardly..."

She raised her hand, eyes sharp at this willful display of temperament. "Dr. Cranshaw is a psychiatrist at the Mental Health

Center. The college pays him a retainer. It will cost you nothing."

"But I don't have a car. I..."

"You can take a taxi, Becca. You can ask a friend to take you, but if you stay in this institution you will go. We will require reports from Dr. Cranshaw. You will be there. Twice a week, Becca. Tuesdays and Thursdays." I nodded. She already had it scheduled? "Your first appointment is at four on Thursday." It could have been worse. It could have been during work. I nodded again.

"You will sign in with the desk and Mrs. Styron every night before 10:30. You will be on number four probation. That is, unless the Tribunal decides differently." Not the Tribunal! I nodded again, but I thought I'd be sick. I kept up my neutral front until she finally left.

Tribunal met every Wednesday night. During lunch Wednesday, Helen, who'd been in the group at the beach, mentioned that she had to appear before Dorm Council for staying out at night without signing out. "How about you, Becca? I heard you've got to appear before the Tribunal. Did you bring back liquor or something?"

"Tribunal?" Corinne was horrified. "Becca, why Tribunal? Helen's only going to Dorm Council." I shrugged and put on my headphones to cut off further conversation.

Corinne was waiting when I came out of the control room. "We're going to the OTI for lunch," she said, tossing my bag to me. "Sam Pritchett is meeting us there."

"I'm not supposed to leave campus, Corinne. I'm not supposed to ride in a car."

She fished around in her pocketbook until she found a scarf and a pair of sunglasses. "We'll sit in the faculty room. No one will say anything." We roared out of the parking lot in the Healey.

Sometimes when I had a little extra money and just couldn't stand cafeteria food another time I went to dinner off-campus at the Varsity for greasy pizza with oregano you could see as well as taste. Having lunch off-campus was usually out of the question. If it hadn't been for the children of dead veterans, I would have had to smuggle food in and keep it in my room.

The dead veterans' children were my saviors. On scholarship, their meals were provided as well as their books. At the beginning of every quarter they were issued little booklets of meal tickets. Whoever decided the amount of tickets each dead veteran's child should get must have been a gigantic person with a huge appetite. Even the boys couldn't eat enough cafeteria food to use up all the tickets. At the beginning of the quarter, the dead veterans' children would sell a five dollar book of meal tickets for three dollars, a real bargain. Just before a major event, however, a homecoming game or a prom, when money was needed, the meal tickets could be had for two-fifty.

The best bargain I ever got was from DeeDee Wiggins' pregnancy raffle. Tall and dark haired, with the flat nasal accent of mountain people, DeeDee had never known her father, who had lost his life in some mudhole in the Ardennes after a leave during which he had impregnated DeeDee's mother. DeeDee was on scholarship, away from home for the first time. When asked she would say, "Ahm majorin' in Education." Then she'd wink.

Nobody was surprised to learn she was pregnant. A foot soldier in the sexual revolution, DeeDee was the only person we knew who was engaged to a dorm. People who knew about such things made arrangements for an abortion. They knew a woman in Tarboro who would do it, but it would cost one hundred and fifty dollars. It was so expensive because the woman was very clean and had access to morphine for pain.

One hundred and fifty dollars was a lot of money, and our floor decided to have a raffle for DeeDee. Her roommate took charge, collecting books, clothing, perfume and meal books. DeeDee herself donated ten mealbooks. On the appointed day the prizes were grouped together, the partial bottles of perfume, a pile of jewelry, another of mealbooks. Tickets were a dollar apiece, and before the drawing began DeeDee had more than enough for the procedure. Girls squealed as each pile was claimed. I won the meal books, twenty-three for a dollar, enough to last almost a year.

DeeDee went to Tarboro with two friends, sleeping in the car on the way home. Once she was settled in her room, our whole wing was careful to be quiet so DeeDee could rest. Just before lights out, while talking with her roommate in the hall, I looked down to see that she had stepped in something that had stained her sock. The offending fluid moved in a little flow beside her foot, across the black rubber tiles of the hall, looking only slightly lighter in color than the tile. As the fibers of her white cotton sock absorbed the liquid, they turned first pink, then darker. I realized that the liquid was red, not black or brown, and that it was coming from under DeeDee's door. Not knowing what to say, I grabbed the roommate's arm and pointed to the bottom of the door. She gasped but managed not to scream. Although she put her finger to her lips, our actions made others in the hall notice and come over, quiet as mice.

We had to push DeeDee out of the way of the door to get it open. Others ran silently for rolls of toilet paper. A nursing student packed her crotch with toilet paper. We put her raincoat on her, taped her waist, arms, and legs to a straight-backed chair, and with five girls on each side we fled down four flights of stairs and across the quadrangle to the infirmary. Her roommate stayed with her while Dr. Steele gave her a cursory look, waiting for the ambulance from Pitt Memorial Hospital.

The emergency room staff and the obstetrician worked long and hard. Early in the morning he came out to tell DeeDee's roommate, "I've got bad news and good news. We lost the baby boy, but the little girl will make it." That's how DeeDee came to be the mother of the female part of fraternal twins.

I almost never ate at the Old Towne Inn, or the OTI as it was known. Even the tuna salad sandwich, the cheapest thing on the menu and my favorite, was out of my league. Corinne swept inside, blew a kiss at the man behind the cash register and said something in either Italian or Greek that made him smile. Taking me by the arm, she guided me into the faculty room.

"You're going to ruin your skin, Becca," Irena Steele said when she saw my tan. She and Dr. Pritchett had glasses of beer in front of them. Though we all knew it was against regulations for a woman student to sit at a table with beer on it, I sat down anyway.

"So, Becca. What's new?" Dr. Steele grinned.

"So," I thought. "Everyone knows."

"Leave the child alone. She'll tell us when she wants to." Dr. Pritchett took a gulp of beer. "How 'bout now, darlin'?"

"There's not much to tell. We all went to the beach, stayed a day longer than we planned, and got caught for not signing out." I shrugged.

"Helen was in the same group, though, and she's just going before the Dorm Council. They're dragging you to Tribunal, Becca." Corinne waited. When I didn't answer she continued, "Trixie Brown is fit to be tied, Becca. We know about this because she called the station. Sam was there. She also called the infirmary. That's how Irena knows. Trixie wants your medical records."

"Trixie! That can't be her name," I said.

"Her name is 'Clarissa', but we call her 'Trixie' because she's such a.., ahhm, dog."

This was another facet of adulthood I hadn't seen before. I had pretty much clumped adults together, much like Mean Jimmy, into groups of either Shitheels or Asswipes. Now it seemed that some of them bridled at having only those two choices. Some of them wanted to help.

"It was a little more than a problem with the sign-in sheet," I began. They nodded, waiting. "When I registered for college I listed my parents as deceased."

"They're not dead, Becca?" Would Corinne be mad and choose one of the two adult groups?

"'Dead' is relative." I was able to say it with a straight face, but they began laughing nervously. I continued, "Some people are born dead and never live, though they exist. Others kind of damp off like seedlings. People's minds die. Some people are born without hearts, or their hearts die later in their lives. That's what happened to my parents. They are dead, really. They're just looking for a place to drop."

They sat stunned at my little speech. "But, Becca,.."

Dr. Pritchett put his hand over Corinne's to stop her. "Darlin', I'm sure you have your reasons for thinking these things. No one has a perfect family."

"What happened when you got back from the beach?" Corinne asked, trying to contain herself. "Did she call you into her office right then?"

I shook my head. "She didn't have to. She was in my room."

"*She was in your room?*"

Her outrage surprised me. "Yeah. She said I was wicked and deceitful. She told me I was on probation and bound over to Tribunal."

"What else?"

Embarrassment made me drop my eyes. "She said that to stay in school I'd have to see a psychiatrist out at the Mental Health Department."

Corinne shook her head, almost forgetting I was there. "I know there are issues that cloud this case, but Becca's civil rights are at stake here." Civil rights? Did they think I was a Negro?

"What do you think about all this, Becca?" Dr. Pritchett asked.

This was taking a turn I hadn't expected. "I don't know what to think. I don't know what you mean. What does this have to do with civil rights?"

Corinne was trying to keep calm, but her emotions were raging. "Becca, haven't you noticed how female students are treated here? There's a double standard. Women have to wear dresses and skirts. Men have no dress code. Women have to tell where they are every moment after five o'clock if they aren't in the dorm. Men come and go as they please. Women aren't even allowed to be at a party or sit at a table where liquor is served. Can you see the men submitting to that? Women are closed out of certain math and science classes. They're discouraged from majoring in certain areas, and actually harassed in classes usually saved for the males. And now you tell us that the Dean of Women was actually in your room! The Bill of Rights must be writhing in agony." Her voice was getting louder.

Irena Steele was nodding as Corinne talked. "Women at this college are treated just like Negroes in the South. Both have been kept ignorant and uneducated, but now both are demanding what is theirs by the Bill of Rights. Women are a part of 'We the People' just like the Negroes, Becca, just like you learned in civics."

If it was hard to keep from cutting my eyes around the group in disbelief before, the comment about civics class was too much. I couldn't suppress a laugh. "In my civics class the teacher passed around a sheet of paper with a picture of an ape on one side and a Negro on the other. It listed the same physical attributes for both."

Corinne and Dr. Steele were incredulous, but Dr. Pritchett was nodding. "I've seen that, Becca. Klansmen circulate that particular piece of trash with regularity."

"What did you do, Becca?" Corinne's voice was softer.

"Do? I passed it to the the student behind me. I was fourteen. I concentrated every fiber of my body, every ounce of willpower into getting out of there." My fingers found the wispy silver cobwebs of scars on my wrists and I rubbed them absently as the group digested this silently.

Finally Dr. Steele asked, "What do you think about the issues we're discussing today, Becca?" She was earnest. Habit was strong. I wanted to play dumb, to avoid the question with a joke, but she really did want to know. "Everything is so relative. This is the first time I've even had any choice about what to study, the first time I've ever had such a good job. I've never had a lock on my door before. I see the inequities you point out, but coming from my end of the scale, the oppression you find so weighty feels easy to me."

Corinne asked, "What about Tribunal tonight?"

The discussion had caused the prospect of that to crystalize in my mind. "Nothing they can do can hurt me, Corinne. I don't date, so that won't bother me. I can still work and go to class. I'm a nobody to them. I don't exactly have a high profile, so they'll forget I'm even alive in a couple of months. If I need to, I'll use the psychiatrist as a buffer between me and my parents. I have eighteen more months of school left. I'll make it."

The adults were staring at their plates. Corinne raised her eyes. "I know you will, Becca."

Sam Pritchett said, "Since I'm the faculty advisor for the Men's Tribunal, Becca, I could be there to interpret the medical records," Dr. Steele offered. "When there's a fracas involving both men and women I often come."

172

"Any faculty member can attend," Corinne added.

I hesitated a moment, thinking fast. Did they want me as a test case, their standard bearer in this civil rights fight? I couldn't take the chance. I didn't have the strength for it.

"Thanks," I told them. "I know you mean well, but I have to trust my own judgment on this. I've got to handle this myself and take the punishment. I'm a quiet person and they'll forget about it soon. They'll leave me alone, and that's fine. I appreciate your interest, though."

The Tribunal saved my case for last. Waiting outside the heavy oaken double doors I heard the voices of girls reciting the Pledge of Allegiance, followed by the Lord's Prayer. I watched girls go in when called. Some walked out with red spots on their cheeks and tight white lips. A few were crying.

I went inside when called and stood in the middle of a horse-shoe-shaped desk. Around the horseshoe sat fifteen girls my age and two older people, one of them Dean Brown. "Trixie," I thought, almost smiling.

The girls around the desk were so much alike they seemed like rooted cuttings from a mother plant. Their clothing was all variations on a theme, shirtwaist dresses and blouses of Madras plaid cotton, not one larger than a size four. Skirts, whether pleated or wrap-around, were all navy blue. Each one wore Weejuns, and a golden pin adorned the exact center of each left breast. These were sorority queens, the cream of cream, the sweethearts of every letter of the Greek alphabet. The whole starved bunch of them hadn't consumed a single unit of complex carbohydrate since pledging their sorority. One girl was supposed to represent the 8,000 non-sorority females at the college, but I couldn't tell which she was. Her left nipple was also capped with a gold pin, perhaps from a fraternity boy. Since this sister barbarian didn't make herself known, I was at the mercy of these other-beings.

I stood before them, feeling lumpy and rotund in my size twelve dress and my ordinary loafers, my left breast pinless and natural in its unpadded cup. "Gulliver must have felt this way," I thought.

One of the diminutive girls read the charges against me, noting that I had never been caught for anything before. My lips almost betrayed me with a smile. "Never been caught," indeed! They obviously assumed I had committed other crimes against the institution. Listening to the litany of transgressions, I thought of all I had really done.

I had tried to be comfortable by wearing clothes other than skirts; attempted expansion of my knowledge by reading books paid for by taxpayers and tuition in an unauthorized place; noticed and commented that the hirelings of the place had the best parking spaces and other amenities, showing how much more they were valued than those of us who paid the bills. My stomach felt queasy and my mind writhed at those thoughts. It wasn't the infliction of pain or the sting of the wound that was so difficult to bear; what cut to the quick was the realization that the self was so unvalued. The Orwellian truth of some animals being more equal than others began to rub salt into the sore.

In a flash I understood how Negroes continued to go to the other water fountain without killing those who had erected the sign. They did it for the same reasons I did not kill my parents before I left. They did not allow themselves to think of the ramifications of dehumanization and inequality. Their minds, like mine, were repelled by the notion, forced away from it as with the force of the two positive ends of a magnet, sliding away from the ideal of wholeness and equality, making oneself safe from the soul-searing pain of the devaluation to something less than equal.

To acknowledge the transgression is the easy part. To acknowledge the humiliation of devaluation, of dehumanization, would vaporize the limits placed on behavior by civilization, allowing a force to be unleashed as sure as gravity, natural as air and as uncontrollable as destiny. Positive and negative ends of the magnet that is humanity would swing together with a resounding smack, making tyrants tremble.

Yet if thoughts like those rose in my mind, I'd have to acknowledge my own dehumanization, to scream out in humiliation, to get up off my knees and know that death itself would be easier than admitting the wrong inflicted on my self.

Calling up an old defense trick, my mind flew out of my body and up to the far corner of the room, up near the picture molding. It stayed there, serene, out of the way of harm, away from the need for equality, safe.

I nodded my guilt at staying out of the dorm without signing out properly and again for staying at an unauthorized place with males present. I was guilty of wearing improper clothes there and being in the presence of beer.

They were working their way down the list of charges to the part that most interested them, the alleged death of my parents. The charge was falsifying records, since nowhere in the book of rules did it state that a student couldn't say her parents were dead. Almost every girl around the horseshoe voiced her horror of my act, the verbiage of denouncement escalating to a fevered pitch by the turn of the last speaker. Each spoke of her sainted parents, some living, a few indeed dead, and how lucky they were to have or have had, such parents. They spoke of their debt to parents and of biblical admonitions to honor them. A few actually shed a tear. I found myself wondering that moisture of any kind could be shed by those tiny bodies.

I knew they were going to throw the book at me. I would get the maximum, but they wouldn't throw me out. I was put on phone restriction, allowed only to talk to my parents. I would not be able to talk to boys, date, or to leave campus except for holidays. I had to see Dr. Cranshaw at the Mental Health Center twice a week until he deemed me cured.

It was almost midnight when they were finished, watching coldly as I left the room, hoping to see my pain at their harsh punishment. I took care to keep my eyes down as I left. Had the snicker I felt bubbled out of me, all would be lost. They must have thought me distraught, letting me leave without comment.

Three long golden boxes waited for me on Daphne's desk back at the dorm. "Technically you ain't supposed to have these, but I figure they got here before you got your sentence," she stated through her gum. Each box was from Blooms, the town's best florist. Each contained twelve long-stemmed red roses. The cards said simply, "Corinne," "Irena," and "Sam."

The roses looked surreal in my bedroom, bare except for the clock and the Motorola. I put each dozen in its own pickle jar and sat them on the window sill for the breeze to carry their scent inside. The golden boxes were elegant to me. I kept them, too.

With the Singer I made myself a tiny, if crude, bathing suit out of the same material as my dress and Corinne's chair. Every spare moment I spent in the sun court studying. Soon my body was mahogany and my grey eyes even paler. I talked to no one, pretending great hurt. People moved to the side when I passed. Everyone had heard that I had to see a psychiatrist.

Tuesdays and Thursdays with Dr. Cranford weren't all that bad. My test batteries had told him of my intelligence, a quality in short supply with most of his clientele and staff. I enjoyed talking with him, but since he was nondirective in his therapy orientation, seldom asking questions, when I stopped talking, conversation stopped.

Toward the end of our eighth month, in a flush of directness, he asked, "What happened, Becca?"

"My father raped me," I told him. "I am a victim of incest."

"All little girls have those kinds of fantasies," he replied.

I reached down for my purse, then stood up and left without a word. I never went back, never heard from him again. Later I heard that he had gone into his office one Sunday morning and shot himself. I felt neither loss nor joy. It was as if I had never known him, that we had spent no time together at all.

10

The Cypress Knee was the only motel in town with air conditioning, and I treated myself. It was on the bypass around Plimpton that carried the log trucks to the paper mill and the out-of-town cars to the beach.

Needing gas, I pulled the Volkswagen in at the Shell station across from the ABC store and the motel. Angeline Peacock and her daughter Crystal still ran the place. Angeline's husband Bill had fallen into the chipper at the mill. All that was left of Bill for Angeline was the rubber heel of his left safety shoe and an insurance policy that would choke a horse.

There was no stopping the chipper. Whole logs of man-sized girth and as long as a living room went into it, spouting out the other end in chips smaller than your palm without slowing the monster down one iota. Bill probably became a light spot in someone's newspaper or a discoloration in a milk carton. Angeline had a funeral, though. She buried the left heel of that safety shoe in a closed coffin from Tucker's Funeral Home.

Angeline gave birth to Crystal exactly eight months and one week after the funeral of the heel of Bill's safety shoe. Fingers flew. People counted backwards in nines and shook their heads. Some said Crystal was small for a full-term infant, but there she was, the spitting image of her mother.

As soon as she could travel, Angeline bundled Crystal up in her new Buick and headed for Florida. Crystal was in her early teens when they returned. Angeline had picked up a love of golf while in Florida. She joined the Plimpton country club with its small but excellent course. Both stayed very tan. Crystal's tan was fashionable, making her blonde hair almost white and her blue eyes a reflection of sky.

Angeline's was not as attractive. Whether it was because of her excess smoking or the fumes from the gas tanks at the Texaco station she had bought on the bypass, pumping the gas herself, the sun turned her the color of fat on a smoked ham, an opaque yellow-orange. Golfing and the work at the gas station kept her trim and in shape, but her strange coloration caused more than one person to stop and look.

Angeline and Crystal were upstanding women, but many of the men they turned down were cruel and started rumors about them. Their Texaco station became known as "Gas and Ass on the Bypass."

I sat in the Volks distractedly watching Angeline pump the eight gallons of regular my tank held. Suddenly a man I had never seen before, but had obviously heard about the registration drive, stepped over the hose from her pump and thrust his head in my rolled-down window.

"Wha'cha doin' here, you nigga-lovin' bitch?" Terrified, I fumbled with the gearshift to get the stick out of my way so I could climb into the other seat and get out of the car. Out of the corner of my eye I saw Angeline pull the nozzle from my tank and point it, still running, at the man.

The flow soaked his left arm and side from his waist down. The fumes overwhelmed him for a moment, then he gasped. Angeline put the nozzle back into the pump and took a box of matches from her pocket. Taking one from the pack, she put it head first on the striking area, holding the head with her thumb. Then she thumped it with her right middle finger.

The match scraped across the bit of sandpaper and flew through the air, unlit, bouncing off the sleeve of the man's gas-soaked shirt. With the air left in his choking lungs he screamed and fell back against the high test pump.

Angeline had another match propped under her left thumb. It flared as it flew toward him, but he rolled almost under my car to avoid it. The match flipped in tiny circles away from the gas puddle and the man in the soaked shirt. It went out before it hit the ground. He half crawled and half ran toward his car.

She took out another match, walking slowly toward him, propping it between her thumb and the striking surface. He streaked her driveway with rubber in his haste to leave, the third match a flaming pinwheel behind him.

Still shaking and speechless, I handed Angeline a five dollar bill through my open window.

"Becca, pull your car over there for the night." She pointed toward the open bay beside the door to her station.

"Why, Angeline?"

"You stayin' over at the Cypress Knee, ain't ya?"

"Yeah."

"Then leave that piece of foreign shit here for the night. Don't park it in front of your room, Becca."

Sweat broke out all over my body. I nodded and drove toward where she was pointing, rolled up the windows and locked it. "Angeline..."

She held up her hand as if to ward me away from her, looking thoughtful for a minute. "They gave me a readin' test the first time I registered to vote. I'll never forget that. It was so Goddamned demeaning. Maybe it'll get better with you kids here to change things, but it ain't gonna be easy." I nodded, waiting for her to continue.

"Becca, you better git the fuck outta here and stay out. I made the mistake of comin' back. You git out and stay out."

"But, Angeline..."

"People need to register everywhere, Becca. You can find somewhere else to do good work. But you gotta leave here."

"Tomorrow." It was a promise to myself as well as to her.

She shook her head, weary. "Wha'cha gonna do tomorrow?"

"I see Aunt Martha Waters tomorrow."

She looked me square in the eyes for an instant. I could see the sclera of hers were yellow. Angeline nodded.

"Then you leave?"

"Then I leave."

She nodded again. "Aunt Martha Waters was with me when I had Crystal. Tore up as I was 'bout Bill and all, I never felt a bit of pain with that ole lady around. I didn't know she was still alive. Give her my regards."

Across the street at the Cypress Knee I slept fitfully and woke early. The Mayflower opened at five. I had forty five minutes before I could get coffee. I waited for a log truck to rumble past on the 64 bypass before crossing to the Texaco station. The windows of my Volks were white with dew, so I took a couple of the blue industrial strength service station paper towels to wipe them outside and inside. I never saw a Bug that didn't fog up inside if there was any moisture at all outside.

I drove down Washington Street, past Winesett Circle and looked to the right where the County Home used to be. It had been torn down years back when private enterprise discovered that there was gold in them old folks and opened private holding areas for old people. The prison, closed in the late forties, was moved away from civilization over toward Burgaw, further back into the swamp. Now each race had its own prison.

An apartment building stood where the Washington County Home used to be. The monogrammed crepe myrtle with its watermelon-colored blossoms was probably chopped down when the big highway was widened. The low hill with the poor folks' graveyard had been graded. A small hospital, ugly as a toad with its flat roof and brick facade, had been built there, its sides and rear cinderblocks painted green. The hospital seemed to hunker in a hole. It was not a pretty sight. Mr. Sexton's store was gone, and in its place was the entrance to a trailer park.

I hadn't planned it, but since I was so close I drove onto the Pines Road and out toward Houghton Hills, the cemetery where my grandmother was buried. The narrow lane winding through the cemetery was paved with tabby, crushed oyster shells, instead of cement or asphalt. The tabby lane would accommodate the Volks, but I parked and walked along through the stillness of the morning, past the graves of whole families who had lived in the area.

I lost my fight with the urge to go look into the vault looming in the mist off to the right. The metal gate of the fence, fashioned like a row of little lances, creaked just as it had when I was a child. I strained to see through the old glass, discolored by age and weather and the smudges from the faces of long-grown children who had also tried to see the woman in the vault. Her father had been a planter, raising indigo and rice, an owner of land near the Pettigrew plantation. She was the only and much-loved child from his cherished wife. On her sixteenth birthday, the planter hired a little orchestra with two fiddlers, and under the blue moon that night she fell in love with one of them.

Her father and his foremen fanned across the plantation to look for them once they realized she was no longer in the ballroom. They found her floating on top of the water of the main canal, dead, her gown caught in briars that grew along the bank, hydrilla in her hair. The fiddler was never found. The heartbroken planter and his wife buried their daughter in the only above-ground crypt the area had ever seen. Even before the planter died, stories of the strange sounds from the mausoleum were already whispered.

On nights of the blue moon, the rare second full moon in a month, they say you can hear the fiddle playing, the swish of brocade and the scuffle of soft kid dancing shoes. They say that, if you dare, you can look through the glass panes on the mausoleum door and see wet footprints on the floor of the crypt and a sprig of hydrilla beside them. The young woman always dances on the nights of the blue moon.

I tried hard to see inside, feeling like an intruder, knowing that I was. When I closed the metal gate it complained again with a little shriek.

My grandparents' graves were near. I didn't bother to follow the tabby lane, but walked along the edges of the family plots, reading the names: Simpson, McNair, Swain, Spruill, Chesson. Then I saw it, a big plain stone, rough-hewn along the back and edge, slick and shiny as mica on the front.

Incised there was the name, "Bass."

The good Southern child in me hesitated briefly, watching for movement that might be a snake. A tangle of wisteria grew in cords, binding the slender slash pine like rigging, growing twenty feet high near the head of the grave site. Off to the right grew a stand of switchcane. If there were snakes, they'd come from there. Even this early in the morning, as warm as it was, the canebreak rattlers could be moving, searching for eggs to swallow and birds to hypnotize and eat. I would be watchful.

The graves below the big stone were both so overgrown it was hard to see which was Grandfather's and which Grandmother's. I studied the ground around the stone for any movement. Seeing none, I leaned over from the waist to see if I could find the slabs with their names. I saw that her grave was on the left side of the headstone.

There, in a tangle of cinqfoil, lay crockery and the glint of a shard of mirror. I knew it would be a cup or a pitcher, and brushed back the hairy little leaves to touch it. With the knuckle of the middle finger I gave it a rap. Nothing moved. No copperhead slithered forth. Carefully, because the pitcher would make a dandy home for a Black Widow spider, I lifted it and looked inside. There were a couple of roly-polys, but they wouldn't hurt me.

It wasn't a large pitcher. Before it had been cracked from the lip to the base it would have held perhaps only four cups, but it wasn't pot-bellied like a teapot. The base was white, with a thickening blizzard of cobalt flowers swirling upward into a mass of solid blue glaze at the top. "A chocolate pot," I said to myself.

I replaced the pitcher in the indention of sandy white soil and combed the leaves and stems of cinqfoil back over it. Nearby lay a pile of mirror shards, then two or three small round ones, nickel-sized, by themselves. I sat back on my heels trying to remember what these things meant. I think I knew at one time, or perhaps cups and pitchers and bits of mirror on a grave were so common that I thought I knew and never questioned it. Sometimes things from one's childhood are like that.

The flat, horizontal stone I was looking for was right there. "Cornelia Barnes, Beloved Wife," it said. I shook my head, disgusted, and tried to think what I would have said of her. Would I say that she sat in the cool light of evening with her hair down, feeding figs to a crazy man while she trimmed his toenails? Would I say that she was an island of sanctuary during a hurricane, hugging an entire community of people to her, providing physical safety as well as sustenance, and wouldn't allow their pets to die? The stone that marked the place where they buried her body was small, with not much room for discourse. Perhaps "Beloved Wife" was enough. Suddenly I could only remember her lying in that casket with her hair permed and polish on her fingernails.

I duck-walked over to the other grave and held back the vegetation to look at the stone. "Luther Lorenzo, Sheriff," it said. At once I was inundated with the aroma of sour-mash. Not that he drank it, but sometimes when he was busting stills it would splash on him. The image of him rose up in my mind, not with form but as a combination of smells. The gaithers that he clumped through the swamps in always smelled like new tires. His jodhpurs smelled of horse sweat and bloodhounds. The white linen suits he wore in summer when he had to go to court smelled faintly of the hot iron and starch. His flat-topped summer straw boater smelled of hair tonic, but no matter what he wore, no matter what the season, he always smelled faintly of sour-mash.

My legs began to feel prickly from restricted blood flow of my crouch. I stood, feeling as though the quick of myself was on the end of a pin being examined by the people I had studied in class. What would they say on my tombstone? I wondered what words were carved into the gravestones of Nietzsche and Kierkegaard. Was it "Beloved Wife"? Was it "Sheriff"? Did someone chisel of Nietzsche, "He Smelled of Hair Tonic and Sour Mash"? Did someone say of Kierkegaard "He Fed Figs The Color of Amber to a Crazy Man in the Cool Evening"? Did they even have stones with words carved on them?

My feet crunched through the oyster shells along the tabby lane back to my car. I knew that Aunt Martha had left the pitcher and the mirrors beside the big stone that said, "Bass." The Mayflower would be open, but I felt nervous and restless. My heart was pounding as I turned the Volkswagen around and drove back toward the city limits. The highway had been widened, lined now with groups of brick ranch houses I didn't remember, but the area was pretty much as it had been when I had left on the bus that day.

Crossing the bridge over Kendricks Creek, I drove off the main highway and onto the asphalt secondary road. Just past a thick grove of pecan trees I saw the white stucco house with the green roof. There were no other cars on the road. No one stirred on the street. It was only a little after five o'clock.

I couldn't help myself. Pushing the gas pedal to the floor I passed my parents' house as fast as I could, slowing only when I reached the schoolyard at the far end of the road. I pulled off into the driveway, shaking so hard I had to stop and regain control.

"Goddammit," I whispered aloud. "Goddammit." I sat back against the seat and took a deep breath. As I drove back past the stucco house the sound of the chain drive of the car seemed overpoweringly loud. Would they hear it? Would the sound betray me? My heart was in my throat.

The part of my mind that deals in reality knew those thoughts were little more than the bears from childhood dreams still hiding under my bed. They had no idea what kind of car I drove. They didn't even know I was in the county or, indeed, where I was. It was not even six o'clock. They were probably still asleep. Even with those logical reassurances, by the time I reached the main highway, I was breathless and dizzy, as if a great weight were pressing down on my chest.

Fifteen minutes later, when I reached the long, flatbed bridge over the Sound, I was still shaky but elated. The constriction in my chest was gone, bears had been banished from under the bed, and I felt as though I had been missed by a big truck that had almost run me down.

I dawdled over breakfast in Edenton. Checkout time at the Cypress Knee was noon. I had plenty of time.

Even a fire-hose shower in a motel room with the air conditioner turned to its coolest setting cannot withstand the heat and humidity of the Coastal Plain for more than two hours. By three o'clock, when I picked up the orchid at the florist, my careful ablutions, meticulous makeup and freshly ironed skirt and plaid Madras blouse had melted like a candle in a Chianti bottle. Like everyone else in that white hot afternoon, I was soggy from the heat and half blind from the reflection of light on the white earth and from the surface of the river.

Standing under a ceiling fan that cut through and mixed the air, gelatinous with the smells of chrysanthemums and carnations, I watched rivulets of humidity on the glass door of the cooler box that held flowers run in a cool line toward the puddle of water on the floor.

Under my sodden blouse a salty cousin droplet formed in the hollow of my throat and, joining other salty droplets, trickled between my breasts and into the band of my bra which was, by now, wringing wet. Droplets formed and fell from the inside bends of both elbows. I extended my arms to look at the creases. Though I had scrubbed my body not three hours before, a roll of dirt had already formed there. I took the compact from my purse and saw another line of dirt under my chin.

"You got 'tater ridges, honey." The florist was behind me.

'Tater ridges! I hadn't heard that term in years. Aunt Martha used to call them that. No 'tater ridge was safe if she was near the bathtub and could reach the soap. She sought them out, scrubbing them from between toes, under the chin and behind the knees. My heart was about to burst. The happiness I felt made my soggy body tingle. I couldn't wait to see her.

There was as much traffic on River Street as it ever gets. Mill workers were on their way through town to their 4-to-12 shift at the Kiekeffer plant. Since I had closed my windows and locked the car while in the florist shop, the car was thirty degrees hotter than the oppressiveness outside. Plimpton's answer to a traffic jam inched along River Street. I held the steering wheel with a Kleenex to keep the black plastic from scorching my fingers. The towel I sat on kept the backs of my thighs from blistering against the seat, but my back was practically unprotected by my drenched shirt.

The mill traffic stayed on River Street as I turned off on Sugah Hill Street. I drove along the packed white hardpan of the road up to the ridge where unpainted houses lined both sides of the street. The yard of 664 Sugah Hill was pretty much like every other yard in that row of houses, except for the two Chinaberry trees in the yard.

Since it was not quite four o'clock, I hesitated a moment, driving to the top of the ridge and turning around. A puzzling shyness gripped me, a feeling of being drawn toward something irresistible, at the same time feeling almost terrified at experiencing it.

Chinaberry trees are not of the same stature as billowing live oaks or sap-oozing loblollies. They hardly ever grow over 25 feet high. Their crowns are naturally umbrella-shaped, with leaves small and dark green, the size and shape of goldfish. In summer, their prolific dun-colored berries drop and cover the earth underneath. The blanket of berries and the dense shade allow little sunshine to nourish grass under a Chinaberry tree. For those reasons, Chinaberries are seldom found in the yards of rich people who have air conditioners instead of shade.

Poor people don't give a damn about grass. They love the shade of the umbrella-shaped trees and the children love the berries. After one bite they learn to keep the berries out of their mouths. The berries can become pulpy projectiles for slingshots and when strung together by little fingers they are necklaces. Adults rake the berries into piles beside the wonderful dense shade the crown bestows and put chairs there in the cool of the evenings. The earth under the trees at 664 Sugah Hill Street was bare and hard. I parked my car in the blessed coolness there.

I walked around to the passenger side and opened the box holding the yellow orchid with the reddish purple lip. I had already tied the silver moon-woman to the silken cord and had made a bow on the slender part of the neck of the blue vase. My hands were shaking again and I was overcome with dread.

"This is so fucking stupid." The thought was so vivid I thought I had said it aloud. For a moment I thought of tossing the vase and flower into the floor of the car and tearing from the yard, but the movement of a curtain caught my eye. I would go inside.

Doctor Grey owned all eighty or ninety houses on Sugah Hill, renting them by the week. No one ever accused him of squandering his money on repairs. The bowed and rotting steps to the sagging porch were only twenty feet from my car, but anxiety made me breathless before I got there.

From navigating the steps of other poor people's houses, I knew to locate the risers and step there, the strongest spot, least likely to collapse under one's weight. The sagging porch was worn smooth by the feet of many occupants and the brooms of countless women. Even in the heat the front door was closed. I knocked lightly and the door opened slowly.

I felt as though I were strangling. I gulped for speech, hoping social grace would save me. "Hello, I'm Becca Bass. I have a four o'clock with Aunt Martha Waters." My face caught fire. Swallowing, I rushed speech again. "I mean, I was told I could see Aunt Martha Waters at four o'clock."

A dusky hand motioned me inside. A soft voice murmured, "Marfa is waitin' fo' you." I put the blue glass vase into the dark hands.

My mouth held too much spit. My teeth seemed to have multiplied. "I brought her this," I managed to mutter.

The pupils of my eyes were pinned closed from the fierce light of the sun outside. I almost stumbled over a dark form sitting beside the door. The woman who took the orchid guided me to an ottoman of yellow plastic and indicated for me to sit. Though my eyes were still adjusting, I was aware of the smell of incense and that there were many people in the room.

My vision cleared with painful slowness. Gradually I saw people sitting in straight-backed chairs along the walls. Two others occupied the three upholstered chairs. Looking to my left to see what caused a little noise, I realized that there was a toilet in the middle of the living room. A puff of breath betrayed my astonishment, and the woman beside me said, "City make de doctah put in plumbin'. He put it in heah."

Another puff of air came out of me. "In all ninety houses?" I whispered.

"He hab ninety-seben."

I nodded and rolled my eyes upward, hoping she'd think I was looking at the metal ring suspended from the ceiling to hold the shower curtain providing privacy for the user of the toilet. I was really trying to keep the tears collecting in the corners of my eyes from moving onto my cheeks.

Blinking quickly, I looked to my right. Without even moving my body, I could see all the way through the house, through all the rooms lined up like a train, all the way out the back door. On a dresser against the wall of the second bedroom I spotted the source of the incense. An ornate altar adorned the dresser. Several cones of incense sent smoke curling to the ceiling. The picture of saints in ornate gilt pressed pasteboard frames were festooned with garlands of herbs and garlic and bones on strings. The scene was so wildly exotic and at the same time so wonderfully comforting and familiar.

The light from the door at the end of the house was cut by figures walking toward the living room. When they came abreast of the altar I saw two large women bearing a chair with a tiny very old woman wrapped in an ornate quilt of velvet and satin patches. They moved through the sultry air, curls of incense smoke following them into the room toward the vacant chair beside me.

I was on my feet, gaping. Seated in the chair borne by the women, she looked like a little potentate. I reached to help them place her in the chair, but they told me with a jerk of their heads that they would take care of it. Gently they moved her to the upholstered chair, placing her swaddled feet on the footstool. One of the women motioned for me to sit back on my ottoman.

The woman holding the blue vase came forward and waited until the tiny woman made a small gesture with her hand. "She brang you dis," she said. Aunt Martha nodded and the bearer of the vase walked into the next room and put it on the altar. I cringed inside myself when I saw it there. All of the other things, the holy objects, on the altar, looked so natural there. They had the symmetry of a vine reaching for the sun, its leaves jockeying for just the right position and presenting a feast for the eye. The cobalt vase with the yellow orchid and the silver moon-woman was cloying and contrived by contrast. I felt sick inside.

One of the bearers of the chair nodded to me and then to Aunt Martha. My God, what would I say to her? I should have thought about it in the motel. I should have made a list. My mind cast about wildly. "Aunt Martha, I'm Becca. Angeline Peacock and her daughter Crystal send their regards." She was sleeping, I thought, thankful. I was so uncomfortable I dared not look up at the women standing beside her for fear of seeing ridicule in their eyes.

When she opened her eyes and looked at me I saw the haze of irises. Her eyes were the same color of blue grey as Captain Sexton's before he died. She was almost blind.

Looking inside myself, remembering her protection and love, I croaked, "Aunt Martha..."

She opened her eyes again and her head jerked back. A sound that was a combination of a gargle and a sniffle came from her. When she moved her head, I could see a silver device in her throat. One of the women who had borne the chair stepped quickly forward with what looked like the bulb on a blood pressure cuff. Her body obscured my view of the procedure, but I heard a gurgling sound.

The floor of the room tipped a little. I thought I would faint. The other woman who carried the chair put her hand on my forearm. "Aunt Marfa breathe through dat pipe in her throat. She had cancer and dey cut out her voice box." The bulb device gurgled again and my stomach churned.

The little girl with eyes like a malamute was pulling at my sleeve. I attended to her. "What kind of Koolade do you want?" she asked. I stared at her. "Orange or grape. We got bof."

"Grape."

In a rush I realized how topsy turvy everything was. What had been reality for me as a child was without substance like the smoke from the incense. Though the thoughts of her power during my childhood had sustained me through the hell of my life with my parents, they were ephemeral.

Aunt Martha had never been just mine. She had her own home, her own family. She had her own friends and sphere of influence. I was but one of many little white children she took care of in the course of her life.

A small cool hand on my bare arm demanded attention again. "Yo want some ice in dat?"

I started to nod. Ice is the sacrament of the South. I never thought about expressing a preference for it, assuming it would be present in any drink served in the summer. The very question made me think about my answer. In the dim room, a naked bulb hung from a ceiling wire. Not a single outlet showed along the baseboard. The only inside light came from the candles at the dresser-top altar. There was no refrigerator in the kitchen. Would there be an ice box? Did the iceman still drive his heavy truck up Sugah Hill? Would these warm, dark people even have the money for ice? "No, thank you. No ice."

People in the room shifted almost imperceptibly. It was the right answer. A little sigh popped out of me as if I had been squeezed.

I looked back at Aunt Martha, sitting there tiny and frail, old and cancer-ridden. She was still the goddess of the room, in her velvet and satin, her thin old skin golden in the candle light. I turned my back on the room. "Aunt Martha..." I couldn't think what to say. Tears were dripping off my jawline.

She opened her eyes and nodded.

The little hand on my shoulder demanded attention again. I wiped my eyes with the back of my hand and turned around. The little blue-eyed girl held out a huge red plastic glass filled with grape Koolade.

Hoping that the etiquette of our different cultures would intersect, or if not, the generous people in that room would understand, I waited to take my first sip until everyone was served. A few of the women got glasses, but most were served their Koolade in Mason jars.

In the dawn of a thought I was back at the end of a furrow of soybeans growing in white sandy soil, a hoe in my hand. In front of me was the five gallon jar half full of ice, the frigid water causing the glass to weep with condensate, one grey and blue speckled dipper inside. They were all waiting for me to drink.

190

I tipped the big red glass. The draught was warm and almost gritty with sugar. The artificial grape taste was nectar to me. "Delicious. Thank you." The little blue-eyed girl beamed. All the women in the room moved a bit again. They nodded slightly to each other from the waist as they drank and murmured.

Aunt Martha's tracheotemy tube began to clog again, but this time it didn't bother me. I watched as the big woman with the bulb suctioned the mucous from the silver opening.

"Do you take care of her? Are you her nurse?"

"It be my turn till midnight. I take care ob Miz Waters till den. Den dey hab a turn." The big woman nodded at the others in the room.

The twenty or thirty women and girls nodded from the waist again, ever so slightly. Candle light reflected from the quick, shy glances of proud eyes and from white teeth that showed themselves in little grins in spite of the owners' efforts.

Warmth and sweetness flowed through me like iceless grape Koolade. The flow of love I had always felt for Aunt Martha joined the tide of love the other women felt. It flowed like a strong but unseen current through the room.

The silence was broken only by the audible breathing of the old woman, fragile as crockery, brittle as a mirror shard.

A twinge of envy, a wrench of regret grabbed at my heart. "I can't stay. I live so far away. I can't take a turn."

For the first time the big woman looked squarely at me, her hooded eyes the color of dark swamp honey. "We all take whatevah turn we kin take," she said, and nodded at the altar in the next room.

Did she want me to pray or something? The little blue-eyed girl slipped her hand in mine and pulled me to my feet. We walked together toward the glow of candles. She stood on tiptoe and slid the vase with the yellow orchid to the right. Candlelight shown through the petals, making it glow like a harvest moon, like Aunt Martha's amber skin. "Miz Waters, she need rent money." The little girl was matter-of-fact about it. She pointed to a half-pint preserves jar beside the smoking incense cones. A couple of dollar bills were curled in the mouth of the jar and some change lay in the bottom.

The big woman was behind me.

"How much is rent a month?" I asked.

"It be nine dollah a week. The doctah go up on rent last month."

Nine dollars a week, forty dollars a month, I thought. My finances were still precarious, but there was no question that the rent would be paid. I would stop at Angeline Peacock's gas station on the way out of town and tell her of Aunt Martha's needs. I put one of my two twenty dollar bills into the potbellied jar.

"I'll send money every month," I told the big woman. "And I'll tell Angeline Peacock out on the bypass to do the same. I'll tell her that if Aunt Martha ever needs money for anything else to expect a call from you." She nodded.

"If..." Tears welled up and halted my voice. "If anything happens to Aunt Martha...I mean, when she dies..." Maverick tears escaped my eyelashes and ran down my cheeks. "Would you call and tell Angeline? She'll let me know." I could hardly talk. The little girl skipped into the living room to get a little pennant of toilet paper for me to dry my eyes on. The big woman nodded again.

"I have to go. I have to say goodbye." I said it to the candles and the altar and the orchid. Holding the little girl's hand again I went back into the living room. I looked around the room at the women standing there. "Thank you for letting me take a turn," I managed to say through my tears. I assumed they all nodded in their graceful swaying way.

I sat down on the edge of the ottoman and put my hand ever so lightly on the velvet and satin quilt. I didn't have to think of what to say. It came from my heart. "I have always loved you," I told the little old woman.

The movement under the quilt was almost undetectable. She moved again and brought her right hand out to rest for a moment on top of the lovely stitching. Dumbstruck, I watched as her fingers began to move. She was spelling with her fingers! She had either picked it up from Grandmother or Grandmother had taught her.

It had been years since I had read finger spelling. I strained to understand.

Slowly, slowly the thin old fingers moved and said to me, "Marry the man with the golden..." The movement was unclear to me.

"Cap? Did she say 'cap'?" Maybe the old woman was joking, teasing me, but it stung me like the snap of a rubber band. "Aunt Martha, you know I'll never marry," I chided. "Not even if he has a golden cap."

The old woman took her hand back under the quilt. A little smile played on her face. The other women were smiling too.

"Miz Waters need to sleep now," the big woman told me.

Standing, I leaned over to kiss her and whispered again, "Aunt Martha, I have always loved you."

To the rest of the women I said, "Thank you for everything." I took the little blue-eyed girl's hand and went through the door she held open. Together we walked to my car.

"She say 'cup,'" the girl said abruptly.

"Cup?"

"Aunt Marfa, when she talk wif her fingers to you, she say 'Marry de man wif the golden cup, not cap." She explained it to me slowly as if to a child.

"Well, whatever," I replied. "I'll never marry a man with a golden anything."

She looked at me with those amazing eyes and smiled.

"What is your name, little girl?"

She held out her right hand and began to spell: B-E-C-C-A.

THE CROSSING PRESS
publishes many books
of interest to women.
For a freecatalog,
please call toll-free

800/777-1048